Wholeness in Every Season

Nurturing Stability Amidst Change

By

Reverend Dr. Sheila D. Salley

USA Writers and Publishers

Endorsements

"Dr. Salley writes with the authority of Scripture and the tenderness of one who has walked through every season she describes. Her insight bridges theology and therapy, offering readers truth with compassion. Wholeness in Every Season will bless every congregation that dares to talk honestly about love, loss, and restoration. This book is both mirror and map—a guide for the soul, and a resource for pragmatic living, and group study."

Bishop Keith W. Reed Sr., Sr. Pastor/Teacher, Sharon Baptist Church, Philadelphia, PA

"Every marriage ministry team needs this resource. Dr. Salley combines scriptural fidelity with compassionate realism. She honors the covenant of marriage while extending grace to those who have known its pain. Through personal testimony and professional insight, she proves that restoration and renewal is still possible. This book will heal hearts and strengthen homes."

Rev. Justin B. Anderson, M.TH, Itinerant Elder, Hickman Temple AME Church, Philadelphia, PA.

*"**Wholeness in Every Season** is a natural extension of Dr. Salley's voice - one shaped by personal experience, grounded in sound counsel, and led by Christ. Her desire to uplift, guide, and bring clarity to others in all relational seasons is evident on every page. I am confident that this work will bless many."*

Stacey C. Lilley, Ph.D., LPSC, LPC-S - Liberty University, Lynchburg, VA

"Dr. Salley speaks as a woman who has lived what she teaches. Her transparency about singleness, marriage, divorce, remarriage and renewal gives permission for others to heal without hiding. She invites the reader to see wholeness not as perfection but as partnership with God's grace. This book is a masterclass in resilience and faith."

Loretta Sweet-Jemmott, Ph.D., FAAN, RN – Villanova University, Villanova, PA

"Working with Rev. Dr. Sheila D. Salley has been a true blessing. Reading ***Wholeness in Every Season*** *deeply impacted my own relationship with God and even strengthened the way I show up in my personal relationships. Dr. Salley writes with warmth, wisdom, and a gentle humor that reflects her kind and compassionate nature. Her guidance brings clarity, hope, and a sense of peace that stays with you long after reading. This book will uplift and transform many lives."*

David Webb, Publishing Consultant

Copyright Page

First Edition — 2025

Printed in the United States of America

Dedication

To my husband, **Harvey**, whose steadfast love, patience, and partnership have reflected God's faithfulness in many seasons of my life.

To my children, **Michael** Franklin and **Ashley Monique**, whose encouragement and laughter remind me daily of God's goodness from generation to generation.

To my extended family, **friends**, and loved ones who have cheered, prayed, and stood by me through life's many seasons—you are living evidence that love endures all things.

To my **interdenominational church family**, thank you for embracing the vision God has placed within me and for demonstrating that unity in Christ transcends traditions and titles. Your prayers, love, and support continue to inspire my walk and my work.

And to every woman and man who has ever wondered if joy could rise again after loss—may this book remind you that God restores, rebuilds, and renews. There is purpose in your pain, beauty in your becoming, and wholeness in every season.

Acknowledgments

First and foremost, I give all glory to **God**, whose unchanging grace has carried me through every word of this work. Without His wisdom, this book would not exist.

To my **family**, thank you for your patience, encouragement, and unconditional love as I devoted countless hours to writing, reflection, and prayer.

To my **mentors and colleagues in ministry and counseling**, your guidance and shared wisdom helped shape the message and clarity of this project. To my **dissertation chair**, Dr. Stacey C. Lilley, your example of scholarship and faith continues to inspire me to teach, lead, and serve with excellence.

To my **church family**, your prayers, encouragement, and consistent faith have surrounded me like a covering of grace. Thank you for believing in the vision God entrusted to me and for reminding me that the Kingdom thrives in unity.

Special thanks to my **Editors, Readers, and Prayer Partners**, whose careful eyes, listening hearts, and honest feedback helped bring this message to life.

And to everyone who has journeyed with me through seasons of change—clients, couples, and congregants—you have all taught me that God's restoration is not theory; it's truth. Thank you for trusting me to walk beside you. You are part of the testimony that *wholeness truly is possible in every season.*

Finally, to every reader who dares to trust God in transition—thank you for allowing me to speak into your life. My hope is that these words bring comfort, courage, and clarity as you discover God's purpose in your own season.

Table of Contents

Endorsements 2

Dedication 6

Acknowledgments 7

Foreword 11

Preface: The Journey Toward Wholeness 12

Introduction: When the Seasons Change but God Remains Constant . 13

Part 1: The Spring and Summer Seasons 14

Chapter 1: The Gift of Becoming 15

Chapter 2: Rooted Before Rising 33

Chapter 3: When Love Takes Root 51

Chapter 4: Weathering the Heat 70

Part 2: The Autumn and Winter Seasons 88

Chapter 5: The Grace to Let Go 89

Chapter 6: The Beauty of Brokenness 108

Chapter 7: Stillness in the Silent Season 126

Chapter 8: When God Heals the Heart 144

Part 3: The New Spring 164

Chapter 9: Love Beyond the Ashes 166

Chapter 10: "Whole and Holy" 185

Epilogue — New Spring: A Season of Renewal 205

Chapter 11: Pastoral Q&A 209

Foreword

It has been a privilege to witness Dr. Sheila Salley's unwavering commitment - not only to her scholarship, but also to the hearts and lives of those she serves. As her dissertation chair, I watched her press forward with deep conviction and resilience, always choosing the path that honored both academic integrity and spiritual calling.

Wholeness in Every Season is a natural extension of her voice - one shaped by personal experience, grounded in sound counsel, and led by Christ. Her desire to uplift, guide, and bring clarity to others in all relational seasons is evident on every page. I am confident that this work will bless many, and I am honored to offer my support. May this book bring light and healing to all who read it.

Stacey C. Lilley, Ph.D. LPSC, LPC-S Counselor Education & Family Studies-Liberty University, Lynchburg, VA

Preface: The Journey Toward Wholeness

There comes a moment in every believer's life when God calls us to look back, not with regret, but with revelation. Each chapter of our story—whether radiant with joy or shadowed by pain—serves a divine purpose. *Wholeness in Every Season* was birthed out of my own desire to understand God's timing in transition: how He restores what's broken, renews what's weary, and refines what's waiting.

For years I counseled others to find peace in God's process, but it was in my own seasons of change that I truly met the Healer. From the anticipation of singleness to the covenant of marriage, from the ache of divorce to the beauty of renewal, God proved faithful. This book is both testimony and teaching—a reflection of lessons learned in tears, laughter, silence, and surrender.

My prayer is that every reader will see themselves in these pages and recognize that God wastes nothing. The same God who ordains spring's beginnings also sustains winter's stillness. Wholeness is not the absence of pain; it is the presence of peace. It is the discovery that grace runs through every chapter and every change.

Introduction: When the Seasons Change but God Remains Constant

Life is never static. The winds of change visit every soul, sometimes with gentle breezes, sometimes with unrelenting storms. Yet through it all, God remains the same. The Bible reminds us, *"To everything there is a season, a time for every purpose under heaven"* (Ecclesiastes 3:1 NKJV). Seasons shift, relationships evolve, and circumstances stretch us beyond comfort—but God's faithfulness never falters.

In this book, we will walk through the seasons of singleness, marriage, divorce, remarriage and renewal. Each represents not only a chapter of life but also a spiritual classroom where God teaches trust, resilience, and grace. As a counselor, pastor, and woman who has lived through each of these transitions, I've learned that wholeness is possible no matter the weather of our souls.

The message is simple yet profound: Wholeness is not found in a specific season—it is found in the Savior who governs them all. When you realize that His presence remains through every change, fear gives way to faith, and despair yields to divine peace. Whether you are basking in the sunlight of fulfillment or standing in the cold of uncertainty, may you come to know this unchanging truth: God is working for your good in every season of your life.

Part 1: The Spring and Summer Seasons

***Spring** reminds us of* becoming. *It is the season of beginnings, where dreams take root and faith blossoms anew. It whispers, "Grow." God invites us to trust the unseen, to plant seeds of obedience, and to believe that what He has promised will bloom in due time. Spring is the reminder that buried things can live again.*

***Summer** teaches us about* sustaining. *It is the season of heat and harvest, of work and reward. It reveals the strength of what has taken root. Even in the warmth of trial, God waters the soil of our souls with grace. Summer says, "Endure." It calls us to faithfulness, to tending what we've planted, and to letting love mature through perseverance.*

Part 1

The Spring and
Summer Seasons

Chapter 1: The Gift of Becoming

"Being confident of this very thing, that He who has begun a good work in you will complete it until the day of Jesus Christ."

— **Philippians 1:6 (NKJV)**

Exegetical Note: Paul's letter to the Philippians was written during imprisonment, yet it radiates joy. The phrase "begun a good work" (Greek: *enarchomai*) means "to initiate with purpose and continue with commitment." Paul reminds the believers that God's work in them was not impulsive—it was intentional.

Historical Context: The church at Philippi was the first European congregation Paul founded (Acts 16). It began with unlikely converts—a businesswoman named Lydia, a freed slave girl, and a jailer—each representing God's inclusive grace.

Pastoral Insight: Becoming is not about doing more; it's about trusting that the God who started your story will finish it beautifully. You are a work in progress—and that's holy ground.

The Sacred Whisper

Every spring carries a sacred whisper: *"Behold, I make all things new."* (Revelation 21:5 NKJV) It is the season of becoming—the time when what was hidden beneath the soil begins to emerge. In our spiritual lives, spring is the awakening of identity, purpose, and self-discovery.

So many rush through this season, longing to be somewhere else—to be chosen, to be married, to be established. But God calls us to *become* before we *belong*. The waiting isn't punishment; it's preparation. Before Adam was given Eve, he was given purpose. He named the animals, tended the garden, and walked with God in the cool of the day. His completeness was rooted in communion before companionship.

Becoming is one of life's most sacred processes. It is the gentle unfolding of who God created us to be, shaped by His hand, refined by His Word, and nurtured through our lived experiences. Every believer is in the process of *becoming*—becoming more like Christ, more aware of purpose, and more settled in the truth that we are fearfully and wonderfully made. There is nothing stagnant about spiritual maturity. God calls us not merely to exist, but to evolve—to be transformed "from glory to glory" **(2 Corinthians 3:18).**

Becoming is not reserved for the young or for those just starting their journey of faith. It is the daily call to those who have walked with God for decades and still find themselves learning to trust His ways. Becoming is not a one-time event but a continuous unveiling—a divine partnership between Creator and creation. The potter's wheel never ceases to spin, and the clay remains pliable only in His hands. As Jeremiah wrote, "So He made it again into another vessel, as it seemed good to the potter to make" **(Jeremiah 18:4).**

Many believers misunderstand this process, assuming that once we reach a certain age, attain a particular title, or secure a stable relationship, our becoming is complete. But spiritual growth is not limited by age or status. Every season of life—whether single, married, divorced, or widowed—offers an invitation to discover another dimension of God's character and His work within us. Even in the waiting seasons, God is working behind the scenes, weaving lessons into our hearts that can only be learned through surrender.

Becoming is also deeply connected to identity. We live in a culture that tries to define us by our relationship status, accomplishments, or failures. But wholeness begins when we understand that our truest identity is found in Christ. The Apostle Paul wrote, "In Him we live and move and have our being" (Acts 17:28). To *become* whole, we must first *be* in Him. The world says we must find ourselves, but the Spirit says we must lose ourselves in the presence of God, allowing Him to reveal who we are.

The Beauty of the Slow Work

Growth takes time. It cannot be microwaved or manufactured. Every root must deepen before fruit can appear. The same sun that warms the soil also exposes the weeds; and the same rain that refreshes also tests the ground. God's process of transformation is often quiet, slow, and sacred.

You may not see progress at first, but faith flourishes in hidden places. The soil of surrender is where God does His best work. Becoming is holy ground because it is where our willingness meets His workmanship.

There is beauty in becoming because it reminds us that unfinished does not mean unworthy. God delights in the process, not just the product.

He is not waiting at the finish line with arms crossed, but walking beside us, shaping our character, refining our motives, and healing our wounds as we journey toward wholeness. Even our mistakes are folded into His purpose, just as Joseph told his brothers, "You meant evil against me; but God meant it for good" (Genesis 50:20).

Becoming requires courage—the courage to let go of what was so that we can embrace what is yet to come. It takes faith to release the familiar and step into the unknown seasons of transformation. Each time we say "yes" to God's pruning, we are saying "yes" to growth. Each time we choose forgiveness over bitterness, humility over pride, and obedience over convenience, we become more aligned with His image.

When we understand that becoming is both a gift and a grace, we stop resisting change and start rejoicing in it. Every challenge, every heartbreak, and every delay becomes part of the holy curriculum of spiritual maturity. Like a seed that must be buried before it can bloom, our lives must sometimes go through seasons of darkness so that God's light can bring forth new life. "Unless a grain of wheat falls into the ground and dies, it remains alone; but if it dies, it produces much grain" **(John 12:24).**

God's process of becoming does not rush. He is not bound by human timelines. What feels like delay is often divine preparation. In our impatience, we want outcomes; in His wisdom, He wants transformation. When we begin to see life through His eternal lens, we realize that even our waiting has purpose. Waiting purifies motives, deepens dependence, and teaches us to rest in His sovereignty.

As we mature in our walk, we learn to appreciate the seasons when God hides us. Hidden seasons are not punishment; they are protection. In obscurity, God develops strength, character, and discernment. When David was anointed, he did not immediately ascend to the throne. He went back to the fields, where his worship and obedience in the unseen places prepared him for public responsibility. Becoming whole, therefore, begins in the private spaces of devotion before it is ever visible to others.

To become whole is to accept God's pace, God's pruning, and God's purpose. It is to embrace every season as sacred, every change as opportunity, and every challenge as preparation. You are becoming the version of yourself that God already sees—mature, grounded, and radiant with His glory.

I've counseled many who see singleness as a season of lack, but it is actually a sacred invitation to fullness. It is in this time that we learn our worth apart from the world's validation. The danger of skipping this process is entering the next season needing someone else to complete what only God can confirm.

David spent his early years tending sheep long before he sat on a throne. Esther was prepared in solitude before she was presented in royalty. Jesus Himself spent thirty quiet years before three years of ministry. Every divine assignment is preceded by a private becoming.

So, if you find yourself in a quiet season, know this: heaven is at work in the unseen. God is growing roots before fruit, depth before display.

Wholeness is not about what happens next—it's about who you're becoming now.

Vignette: The Runner Who Slowed Down

David was a marathon runner. Every morning before sunrise, he hit the pavement—mile after mile, chasing new records. He thrived on progress, and slowing down felt like failure. But one summer, an injury sidelined him. The doctor said it would take months to heal.

Rest was foreign to David. He sat on the porch in the early mornings, watching other runners pass by. Each footstep on the street felt like a reminder of what he couldn't do. Frustration gave way to prayer, and prayer became revelation.

One morning, as he watched the sunrise, he heard God whisper, *"Becoming isn't about speed—it's about surrender."*

Over the next few weeks, David began journaling instead of running. He prayed longer, listened more, and discovered a deeper rhythm than the one his feet had known. When he finally returned to the track, his pace was slower—but his peace was greater.

Months later, as he crossed the finish line of his first race after recovery, he didn't raise his arms in victory. He bowed his head in gratitude. He finally understood: becoming is not what we achieve, but what God shapes in us while we're waiting to move again.

Reflection: The Beauty of Slow Growth

The temptation to compare your journey to someone else's is one of the greatest thieves of peace. But becoming cannot be measured by human standards. A tree and a rose do not grow at the same pace, yet both fulfill their purpose. The Lord reminds us that *He* determines the timeline for transformation. Every delay is divine development.

Perhaps you're still waiting on a promise, a promotion, or a prayer to be answered. Take heart—the pause is not punishment. God is perfecting what concerns you. Your responsibility is faithfulness; His is fulfillment. What seems small today will stand tall tomorrow if you remain rooted in His Word.

When you begin to appreciate the slow beauty of God's timing, you'll find peace in progress instead of frustration in process.

Life Application: Becoming in Daily Life

1. **In your relationships:** Choose growth over comfort. Ask yourself, *Am I becoming more patient, more forgiving, more Christlike?*

2. **In your purpose:** Stay teachable. Even your expertise is a classroom when God is the Teacher.

3. **In your emotions:** Let go of guilt about where you are. You are not behind; you are becoming.

4. **In your prayer life:** Ask God to show you where He is stretching you rather than where you feel stuck.

5. **In your self-image:** Speak life to yourself. Replace "I'm not there yet" with "God's not finished yet."

When you align your thoughts with His truth, becoming becomes a joy instead of a job.

Closing Prayer

Heavenly Father, Thank You for the gift of becoming. Help me to see Your hand in every transition and to trust you're timing in every delay. Remind me that even when I cannot see the full picture, you are shaping me for something greater. Teach me to yield to Your process with patience and joy. Let my life reflect Your image more each day. In every season—spring, summer, autumn, and winter—help me to become all that You've destined me to be. In Jesus' name, Amen.

Appendix A — Devotional Companion: The Gift of Becoming

"Being confident of this very thing, that He who has begun a good work in you will complete it until the day of Jesus Christ." **(Philippians 1:6 NKJV)**

Purpose of This Devotional:

This seven-day journey deepens your understanding of what it means to become. Each day invites reflection, prayer, and practice—helping you move from reading to transformation. Becoming is not a single event; it is a rhythm of surrender and growth.

Day 1 — Planted on Purpose

Scripture: Jeremiah 29:11

Reflection: Even when you can't see what God is doing, He has planted you with purpose. Seeds don't sprout overnight—they surrender to the soil first.

Practice: Write one area of your life that feels buried. Pray, "Lord, help me trust the ground You've placed me in."

Prayer: God, give me grace to rest where You've planted me, believing that growth is already underway.

Day 2 — When Progress Feels Slow

Scripture: Galatians 6:9

Reflection: Slow progress is not wasted progress. God is forming patience in the waiting.

Practice: Note one place you've seen small signs of growth in the past month. Celebrate it as evidence of grace.

Prayer: Father, remind me that delay does not mean denial. Strengthen me to keep sowing faithfully.

Day 3 — Surrendering the Timeline

Scripture: Ecclesiastes 3:1

Reflection: Every season under heaven has divine timing. When we release our expectations, peace follows.

Practice: Surrender your current timeline to God. Write: "Lord, I release my 'when' to Your will."

Prayer: Teach me to live in rhythm with You, not my calendar.

Day 4 — Becoming Without Comparison

Scripture: 2 Corinthians 10:12

Reflection: Comparison steals joy and distorts perspective. Your journey doesn't need to look like anyone else's.

Practice: Identify one person you've compared yourself to. Thank God for their path—and yours.

Prayer: Help me find contentment in my calling and confidence in Your craftsmanship.

Day 5 — Lessons from the Runner

Scripture: Hebrews 12:1–2

Reflection: True endurance begins when we stop running for applause and start running toward purpose.

Practice: Reflect on the 'Runner Who Slowed Down.' What part of his story mirrors your own pace?

Prayer: Jesus, be my focus when I'm tempted to rush. Teach me to run the race set before me with grace.

Day 6 — Rooted in Relationship

Scripture: John 15:4

Reflection: We grow best when we stay connected to the Vine. Becoming isn't about effort—it's about abiding.

Practice: Set aside 10 minutes for quiet prayer or worship. Listen more than you speak.

Prayer: Lord, help me stay close to You. Let every branch of my life bear fruit that honors You.

Day 7 — Becoming Whole

Scripture: Romans 8:28

Reflection: God weaves every moment—joy and pain—into His masterpiece. Wholeness is the reward of surrender.

Practice: Journal three ways you've changed since this season began.

Prayer: Thank You, Father, for shaping me into who You designed me to be. My becoming belongs to You.

Becoming is not simply a spiritual journey—it is also an emotional and psychological one. In counseling, I've learned that the greatest barrier to "becoming" is often the narrative a person carries within. Scripture tells us that God initiates a good work within us (Philippians 1:6), but many believers silently battle internal dialogues that deny that truth.

Below are the core counseling principles that support the process of becoming:

Pastoral Counseling Lens - From the Counseling Chair

Cognitive Reframing: Renewing the Inner Dialogue

One of the foundational tools in Christian counseling is reframing—challenging the internal narratives that distort God's truth. Many individuals say:

- *"I'm not enough."*

- *"I should be further along by now."*
- *"If I were valuable, someone would have chosen me already."*
- *"I've missed my moment."*

These thoughts create emotional paralysis. They elevate timelines over transformation.

Paul encourages us, "Be transformed by the renewing of your mind" (Romans 12:2). Renewing the mind is not merely thinking positive thoughts; it is replacing *falsehood* with *biblical reality.*

Counseling Reframe:

Instead of "I'm behind," the truth becomes:
"I am becoming in God's timing, not mine."

Instead of "I'm not chosen," the truth becomes:
"I am already chosen by God (1 Peter 2:9)."

Instead of "I should be married by now," the truth becomes:
"God is developing me for the season He has prepared."

Instead of "I keep failing," the truth becomes:
"Every step, even the painful ones, is part of my transformation."

Reframing does not dismiss pain; it redirects perspective so the believer can see grace where they previously saw guilt.

Attachment Insight: Becoming Whole Before Belonging

Much of becoming relates to emotional attachment styles formed early in life. Many adults unknowingly interpret God through the lens of their earliest relationships.

- Anxious attachment says: *"I must perform to be loved."*
- Avoidant attachment says: *"I must protect myself from vulnerability."*
- Disorganized attachment says: *"Love is unpredictable, so I cannot rely on it."*

But secure attachment says: *"I am loved because love Himself lives in me (1 John 4:16)."*

Becoming requires allowing God to rewrite attachment wounds. You learn that:

- God's love won't withdraw when you struggle.
- Your worth isn't tied to someone's presence or absence.
- Relationships don't complete you—they complement the work God is already doing.

Before Adam received Eve, he received identity, purpose, and communion with God. This order is essential:

- Identity before intimacy.
- Purpose before partnership.
- Wholeness before union.

Forgiveness Work: Letting Go of the Old Narrative

Many people remain stuck in who they *were* because they haven't forgiven:

- Themselves,
- Someone who hurt them, or the season that disappointed them.

Forgiveness is a spiritual discipline, but it is also therapeutic release. Jesus said, "You shall know the truth, and the truth shall make you free" (John 8:32). Forgiveness is agreeing with God's truth rather than the emotional residue of old wounds.

In counseling, I help individuals forgive by exploring:

- The story they told themselves about the wound
- How the wound shaped their identity
- The lies the wound whispered
- The truth God declares over them now

Forgiveness is not excusing the offense—it is releasing the hold it had on your becoming.

Emotional Regulation: Learning to Sit with the Process

Becoming often triggers emotions people try to avoid:

- Frustration,
- Impatience,

- Loneliness,
- Grief over what never happened,
- Disappointment in oneself.

Rather than suppress these emotions, becoming invites you to **notice them, name them, and nurture them under God's care.**

David modeled this when he poured out his soul honestly before the Lord in the Psalms. Regulation does not mean lack of emotion; it means emotions do not run the narrative.

Through prayer, journaling, breath work, and reflection, individuals learn how to:

- Pause instead of panic,
- Reflect instead of react,
- Surrender instead of spiral, and trust instead of forcing outcomes.

The Scriptural Anchor: Becoming Through the Word

Every therapeutic principle finds its grounding in Scripture:

- **CBT Reframing** → "Bring every thought into captivity" (2 Corinthians 10:5).

- **Attachment Repair** → "Underneath are the everlasting arms" (Deuteronomy 33:27).

- **Forgiveness Work** → "Forgive as Christ forgave you" (Colossians 3:13).

- **Emotional Regulation** → "Be still and know" (Psalm 46:10).
- **Identity Formation** → "You are God's workmanship" (Ephesians 2:10).

Becoming is a therapeutic journey because it is first a spiritual one. Transformation happens as the believer learns to align heart, mind, and spirit with the rhythm of grace.

Pastoral Summary

From the counseling chair, I see "becoming" as the sacred intersection of:

- Psychological growth,

- Emotional healing, Spiritual formation, and biblical truth.

- You don't become by striving—you become by surrendering.

- You don't grow by rushing—you grow by resting.

- You don't flourish by comparison—you flourish by connection with God.

- Becoming is the lifelong invitation to allow God to complete the work He began in you.

Declaration:

I am becoming.

Not because I strive, but because God is still working.

My roots are deep. My heart is open.

I am growing in grace and becoming whole.

Closing Benediction for the Week:

"And the God of all grace, who called you to His eternal glory by Christ Jesus, after you have suffered a while, perfect, establish, strengthen, and settle you." **(1 Peter 5:10 NKJV)**

Chapter 2: Rooted Before Rising

"Blessed is the man who trusts in the Lord, and whose hope is the Lord. For he shall be like a tree planted by the waters, which spreads out its roots by the river, and will not fear when heat comes; but its leaf will be green, and will not be anxious in the year of drought, nor will cease from yielding fruit."
— **Jeremiah 17:7- 8 (NKJV)**

Exegetical Note:

In this text, Jeremiah contrasts the life of those who trust in man versus those who trust in God. The Hebrew term for *"planted"* (*shāthal*) means "to transplant" or "to position with purpose." It implies that God Himself is the Gardener who selects the soil, ensuring that your placement is not random but redemptive. The roots symbolize spiritual dependence — unseen but sustaining.

The word *"trust"* (*bāṭaḥ*) conveys a confidence so secure it eliminates fear. This trust isn't passive—it's the posture of one anchored in divine faithfulness.

Historical Context:

Jeremiah delivered this prophecy during Judah's spiritual drought — a time when the people had turned their hearts to idols, trusting alliances and appearances over God's promises. In this warning, he paints a vivid agricultural metaphor: two kinds of lives—one cursed, one blessed. The blessed life is not immune to drought, but it survives it.

Just as the River Jordan nourished the land even in arid times, God's Spirit nourishes His people beneath the surface of visible circumstance.

Pastoral Insight:

Before God raises you, He roots you. Many want elevation without depth, visibility without stability, and fruit without formation. Yet every spiritual drought reveals whether we're planted by emotion or by covenant. Growth is never wasted in obscurity—it's preparation for longevity.

So, if you feel hidden or still, take heart. God is not withholding movement; He's developing maturity.

Root deep. Rise strong. Remain fruitful.

Before a tree grows tall, it must first grow deep. The unseen roots are what sustain the visible strength. *"He shall be like a tree planted by the rivers of water, that brings forth its fruit in its season"* (Psalm 1:3 NKJV).

In counseling sessions, I often remind clients that emotional maturity is the spiritual root of healthy relationships. Without it, even good beginnings can wither under pressure. You cannot rise higher in life than you are grounded in truth.

Being "rooted" means developing stability in faith, character, and identity before the tests of life arrive. Too many try to build connection without first establishing conviction. True wholeness grows underground—where no one applauds, but God affirms.

Jesus described this beautifully in the Parable of the Sower (Matthew 13). Some seeds sprang up quickly but had no depth, so when the sun rose, they withered. That "sun" is life's testing, revealing whether our faith is surface-level or soul-deep.

Every tree that stands tall began with a seed hidden beneath the soil. Before it could stretch toward the sun, it first had to grow roots deep enough to sustain the weight of its branches. Likewise, in our spiritual lives, God calls us to be *rooted before rising*. It is a reminder that true growth begins underground—where no one applauds, where no spotlight shines, where only faith and perseverance keep us anchored.

We often desire elevation before preparation. We long to stand where others can see the fruit, but God is more concerned about what's beneath the surface. The unseen determines the strength of what will be seen. Without roots, any wind can topple what we've built. Paul urged believers to be "rooted and built up in Him and established in the faith" (Colossians 2:7). He understood that stability in Christ is not optional—it is essential.

When we are rooted in Christ, we draw nourishment from His Word. Our strength doesn't depend on changing circumstances but on the constancy of His presence. Like a tree planted by the rivers of water, we bear fruit in due season and do not wither under pressure (Psalm 1:3). Being rooted means developing spiritual disciplines that anchor the soul—prayer, worship, study, and obedience. These practices form the unseen roots that prepare us to withstand life's storms.

But being rooted also means enduring seasons when growth feels slow or invisible. God often buries us in the soil of obscurity to prepare us for future visibility. The seed that refuses the soil will never know the joy of fruit. Jesus said, "The one who hears the word and understands it… indeed bears fruit and produces" (Matthew 13:23). Understanding God's process keeps us from uprooting ourselves too soon. Growth requires stillness. Depth comes before height.

Many believers want to *rise* in ministry, marriage, or leadership before they have learned to be *rooted* in humility, patience, and integrity. But elevation without foundation leads to collapse. God's love for us is so complete that He will delay our public rising until our private roots are strong enough to hold the blessing. If He gave us visibility before maturity, the weight of success could crush what hasn't been fortified by surrender.

Roots are also where transformation begins. It's in the quiet places of reflection, repentance, and healing that we are made whole. The deeper the roots, the wider the reach. When God restores our foundations—our mindset, our faith, our understanding of self-worth—He prepares us to rise with purpose. Isaiah declared, "They shall be called trees of righteousness, the planting of the Lord, that He may be glorified" (Isaiah 61:3). God takes pride in His plantings; He rejoices in those who remain steadfast even when growth seems delayed.

Rooted believers are not swayed by trends, opinions, or opposition. They know that roots must go deep to draw from living water. When trials come, their faith doesn't falter, because their confidence rests not in circumstances but in the unchanging God who planted them. To be rooted before rising is to trust God's process even when it is not comfortable.

Being rooted also means releasing toxic soil—old patterns, relationships, and mindsets that stunt growth. Just as gardeners prune diseased roots to preserve the tree, God removes what contaminates the soul. Pruning may feel like loss, but it is an act of divine love. Jesus said, "Every branch that bears fruit He prunes, that it may bear more fruit" (John 15:2). Pruning seasons are often painful but purposeful; they clear the way for healthier growth.

Once our roots are strong, rising becomes inevitable. You do not have to force what God has ordained. When a tree's roots are deep, its rise is natural. You may not see the full manifestation yet, but the same God who planted you will ensure that you rise in His appointed time. Trust His process—He is not withholding blessings; He is fortifying you to sustain them.

In relationships, ministries, and life's calling, being rooted before rising guards us from premature exposure. It ensures that when we rise, we rise whole, balanced, and ready to bear fruit that remains. You are not buried; you are being planted. And the same God who allowed you to go deep will cause you to go high.

Spring is not just for blooming—it's for building strength. It's the season when God asks, *Will you trust Me before I show you fruit?* When we allow the Holy Spirit to anchor us in His Word and will, we won't be swayed by the storms that come later.

Vignette: The Cedar That Waited

Kevin was an ambitious young minister. He preached passionately, led diligently, and dreamed of pastoring his own church. Yet every door he knocked on seemed to remain closed. Frustrated, he once told his mentor, "I feel buried, unseen, and forgotten."

His mentor smiled and said, "Do you know why God made the cedar of Lebanon the strongest tree in Scripture? Its roots grow downward for years before it ever reaches upward. While others sprout quickly, the cedar waits—and then stands for centuries."

Years later, Kevin understood. In the season of being hidden, God had been preparing his heart for humility, empathy, and endurance. When the opportunity finally came, he rose—not with impatience, but with integrity.

The cedar that waited became the cedar that lasted. And so will you. What feels buried now will one day stand as evidence that your roots went deep enough to sustain what God planned for your rise.

Reflection: The Hidden Strength of Roots

It is easy to celebrate fruit but forget the faith that formed it. The root is the most overlooked part of any plant, yet it determines survival. In our lives, roots represent prayer, humility, and dependence on God. These unseen disciplines sustain us when public applause fades.

Ask yourself: *What sustains me when no one is watching?* The answer reveals where your roots are. When your stability comes from intimacy with God rather than approval from people, you can weather any storm. God's most faithful servants have learned that the deeper the root, the steadier the rise.

Roots grow in silence. Depth is formed in devotion. The more grounded you become in God, the higher you can safely rise.

When we value depth over display, we begin to understand the peace that comes from unseen strength.

Life Application: Planting for Spiritual Depth

Protect your root system. Guard your prayer life, your time in the Word, and your mental health. Neglect in these areas leads to spiritual drought.

Evaluate your soil. Surround yourself with people and environments that nourish faith, not drain it. Growth requires godly community.

Be patient with the process. Trees don't grow overnight—and neither does purpose. Trust that unseen seasons are still sacred.

Stay teachable. Rooted people are not resistant to correction. They know pruning is part of progress.

Celebrate quiet growth. Not every season is about blooming; some are simply about deepening. Rejoice even when no fruit is visible.

Closing Prayer:

Heavenly Father,

Thank You for teaching me that enduring growth begins with being grounded in You. Help me to wait with trust, not anxiety. For those who feel unseen or overlooked, let their roots grow deep in Your truth. For those preparing for the future, establish them with patience and wisdom. Uproot fear, comparison, and impatience, and plant stability, discernment, and quiet confidence. Let my life bear fruit in every season because it is firmly rooted in You. In Jesus' name, Amen.

Appendix B — Devotional Companion: Rooted Before Rising

"Blessed is the man who trusts in the Lord, and whose hope is the Lord. For he shall be like a tree planted by the waters, which spreads out its roots by the river, and will not fear when heat comes."
— Jeremiah 17:7–8 (NKJV)

Purpose of This Devotional

Rootedness is about surrender, strength, and unseen stability. Each day will help you draw nourishment from Scripture and deepen the foundation of your faith.

Day 1 — Planted, Not Buried

Scripture: Psalm 1:3

Reflection: God's planting is protection. The soil that feels heavy is the place where your roots are growing strong.

Practice: List one "buried" area in your life that God may be protecting, not punishing.

Prayer: *Lord, help me trust that You have not forgotten me in the soil; You are forming me for fruitfulness.*

Day 2 — The Hidden Work

Scripture: Colossians 2:6–7

Reflection: True strength is developed in secret. Roots grow in quiet obedience, not public applause.

Practice: Take a moment of silence today. Let your stillness be worship.

Prayer: *God, remind me that hidden seasons are holy seasons.*

Day 3 — When Growth Is Slow

Scripture: Isaiah 40:31

Reflection: Waiting is not wasted when it's wrapped in worship. Growth happens beneath patience.

Practice: Spend five minutes writing what you've learned in waiting.

Prayer: *Father, thank You for teaching me endurance. Strengthen my roots until they reach living water.*

Day 4 — Watered by the Word

Scripture: Ephesians 5:26

Reflection: Scripture keeps the soil of our hearts soft and receptive. Without it, roots dry up.

Practice: Read one Psalm aloud. Let its rhythm water your spirit.

Prayer: *Jesus, wash my heart with Your Word today; let truth refresh me.*

Day 5 — Trusting the Soil

Scripture: Proverbs 3:5–6

Reflection: Faith is learning to stop digging up what God is growing. Trust that the ground you're in is ordained.

Practice: Pray, "Lord, I trust the soil You've placed me in." Write what that soil represents in your life.

Prayer: *Even when I can't see progress, I trust Your process.*

Day 6 — Deep Roots in Community

Scripture: Hebrews 10:24–25

Reflection: Strong trees grow together. God never designed you to thrive in isolation.

Practice: Reach out to one person who strengthens your faith. Encourage them today.

Prayer: *Thank You, Lord, for those who water my faith and help me stand tall.*

Day 7 — Ready to Rise

Scripture: 1 Peter 5:6

Reflection: When roots are ready, elevation comes naturally. Humility anchors you for promotion.

Practice: Write: "Lord, when You lift me, keep me grounded in grace."

Prayer: *May my rising reflect Your righteousness, not my résumé.*

Deep roots are not formed in moments of excitement, but in seasons of consistency, stillness, and surrender. In counseling, I often remind individuals that what they interpret as stagnation may in fact be divine strengthening. The unseen work God does in the heart is often the most critical groundwork for emotional, relational, and spiritual stability.

Pastoral Counseling Lens - From the Counseling Chair

Below are the core counseling principles that illuminate what it means to be rooted before rising:

1. Attachment Security: Stability Beneath the Surface

Attachment theory teaches us that stable relationships grow from secure foundations. Spiritually, Christ is our secure attachment—steady, present, unchanging.

Many believers attempt to build relationships on unstable soil:

- Unresolved trauma
- Inconsistent self-worth
- Emotional abandonment wounds
- Fear of rejection
- Internalized shame

But Scripture anchors us: **"You shall be like a tree planted by rivers of water…"** (Psalm 1:3).

To be *planted* means:

- God stabilizes us before He grows us
- God heals us before He reveals us
- God roots us before He raises us

A person who is not rooted will seek validation rather than value, proximity rather than purpose, and affection rather than identity.

Becoming rooted is God's way of protecting us from emotional dependency and relational instability.

2. Cognitive Reframing: Deep Work Over Visible Results

Cognitive Behavioral Therapy (CBT) teaches that feelings follow thoughts. When individuals believe God is silent or distant because life is slow, their emotions follow:

- *"Nothing is happening."*
- *"I'm wasting time."*
- *"Everyone else is growing but me."*

But growth does not always announce itself.

Counseling Reframe:

Instead of "I'm stuck," the truth becomes: *"God is strengthening my foundation."*

Instead of "Nothing is happening," the truth becomes: *"Something is happening beneath the surface."*

Instead of "I should be further along," the truth becomes: *"God is preparing me for weight I cannot yet see."*

A mature believer learns to affirm unseen progress. Spiritual roots develop before spiritual fruit becomes visible.

3. Emotional Regulation: Learning to Honor the Slow Seasons

Rooting seasons often feel emotionally uncomfortable because:

- Progress is invisible,
- Answers seem delayed,
- And prayers appear unanswered.

In counseling, I encourage individuals to practice **emotional grounding**—techniques that bring the mind back to truth when the heart feels overwhelmed.

This includes:

- Breath prayer ("Lord, anchor me.")
- Journaling emotional triggers
- Naming feelings without shame
- Replacing panic with prayer
- Leaning into community support

Rootedness requires *emotional stillness*—the ability to pause without panicking, to wait without worrying, and to trust without trembling.

"Be still and know..." (Psalm 46:10) becomes a spiritual grounding practice.

4. Forgiveness and Pruning: Releasing What Drains the Roots

Healthy roots cannot grow in contaminated soil.

Sometimes individuals are not lacking growth—they are carrying:

- Emotional toxins,
- Old grievances,
- Relational wounds,
- Self-blame,
- Or stale expectations.

Jesus teaches that the Father prunes the branches that do not bear fruit—not to punish, but to prepare **(John 15:2).**

Forgiveness is part of pruning:

- Forgiving yourself for what you didn't know then.
- Forgiving others who damaged your trust.
- Forgiving seasons that seemed wasted.

When bitterness is removed, nourishment returns. When resentment is released, peace flows again.

Forgiveness clears the soil so roots can breathe.

5. Identity Formation: Rootedness Before Responsibility

Many people desire platforms, positions, or partnerships before they develop identity. But spiritual maturity grows from the inside out.

Rootedness reshapes identity:

- You stop reaching for affirmation—because you're affirmed in God.
- You stop fearing rejection—because you're accepted in the Beloved **(Ephesians 1:6).**
- You stop striving to be chosen—because you're already appointed **(John 15:16).**

Identity is not shaped in visibility. Identity is shaped in obscurity.

God cultivates you in hidden places so your future responsibilities do not crush what your character cannot sustain.

6. Scriptural Anchoring: Roots Grow Through the Word

Every emotional and psychological principle in this chapter is anchored in Scripture:

- **Attachment Security** → "Underneath are the everlasting arms." (Deut. 33:27)

- **Cognitive Reframing** → "Set your mind on things above." (Col. 3:2)

- **Emotional Regulation** → "Let the peace of God rule…" (Col. 3:15)

- **Pruning & Forgiveness** → "He prunes…that it may bear more fruit." (John 15:2)

- **Identity Formation** → "Rooted and built up in Him." (Col. 2:7) Rootedness is an act of trust that God is working in the depths of your being—even when your life appears still on the surface.

Pastoral Summary

From the counseling chair, **rootedness is emotional, spiritual, and psychological grounding.**

It is:

- Learning to rest in God's pace,
- Understanding your identity in Christ,
- Releasing what once held you hostage,
- Strengthening your inner life, and
- Preparing for elevation that won't uproot you.

Roots grow slow but strong. And only the rooted can rise without falling.

Declaration:

I am rooted in Christ.

My faith is deep, my trust secure.

I am planted by rivers that will never run dry.

When I rise, I will rise in His strength.

Closing Benediction for the Week

"The Lord will guide you continually, and satisfy your soul in drought, and strengthen your bones; you shall be like a watered garden, and like a spring of water, whose waters do not fail."

— **Isaiah 58:11 (NKJV)**

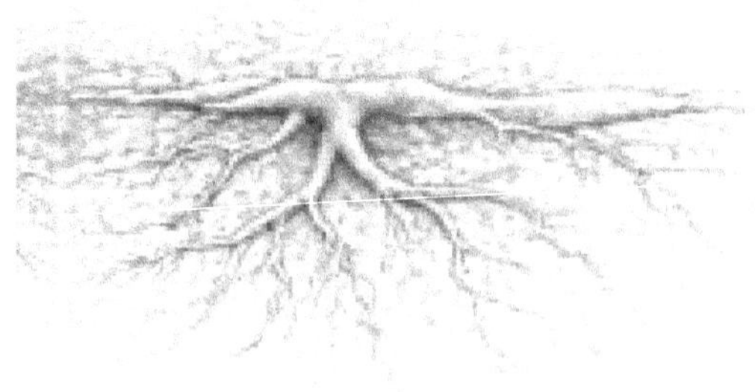

Chapter 3: When Love Takes Root

"Love suffers long and is kind; love does not envy; love does not parade itself, is not puffed up; does not behave rudely, does not seek its own, is not provoked, thinks no evil; does not rejoice in iniquity, but rejoices in the truth; bears all things, believes all things, hopes all things, endures all things. Love never fails."

— 1 Corinthians 13:4–8 (NKJV)

Exegetical Note:

Paul's description of love in this passage uses the Greek word *agápē* — a self-giving, covenantal love rooted in divine character rather than emotion. The phrase *"suffers long"* (*makrothumeō*) literally means "to remain steadfast under provocation." It's love with endurance — a love that stretches without snapping.

When Paul writes that love "never fails" (*oudepote piptei*), the verb *piptō* means "to fall away" or "to collapse." In other words, real love doesn't quite underweight. It matures under pressure.

This is not romantic idealism; it's redemptive realism — love that mirrors God's patience with humanity.

Historical Context:

Paul wrote these words to a fractured church in Corinth — a community gifted but divided, eloquent but immature. They prized spiritual gifts over spiritual fruit. In addressing their conflicts, Paul defines love not as sentiment but as structure — the very framework that holds relationships, families, and ministries together.

The Corinthians lived in a city famous for commerce, art, and moral compromise. Against this backdrop, Paul's words echo loudly: love is countercultural. It does not parade or perform; it persists and protects.

Pastoral Insight:

When love takes root, it grows past convenience into covenant. It learns to bend in storms but never break. Many marriages, friendships, and ministries fail not because they lacked passion, but because they lacked patience. Passion ignites love; patience anchors it.

Rooted love does not depend on feeling appreciated — it draws life from being connected to the Source. It prays when hurt, serves when weary, forgives when forgotten, and still bears fruit in dry seasons.

Love that is rooted in God will always outlast the storm.

Summer arrives with warmth and promise. It's the season of growth, of nurturing what was planted. For those in marriage, it's the time of tending to what God has joined together. *"Therefore, what God has joined together, let not man separate"* (Mark 10:9 NKJV).

When love takes root, it grows from a seed of divine intention rather than mere emotion. It is not rushed, forced, or fabricated. True love, the kind that mirrors the heart of God, begins beneath the surface—quietly, patiently, and prayerfully. Before love can flourish between two people, it must first be grounded in the love of God. For "God is love, and he who abides in love abides in God, and God in him" (1 John 4:16).

Many enter relationships looking for completion, but love that takes root in Christ begins from *wholeness*, not *void.* When we attempt to build intimacy upon insecurity, the relationship becomes fragile—easily shaken when tested by life's winds. But when love is rooted in faith, grace, and truth, it becomes resilient, steady, and fruitful through every season.

The soil of lasting love is spiritual maturity. It takes time for two people to learn the rhythm of grace that sustains covenant relationship. Real love is not proven in moments of romance but in moments of restraint, forgiveness, and perseverance. Paul wrote, "Love bears all things, believes all things, hopes all things, endures all things" (1 Corinthians 13:7). That kind of love cannot survive in shallow soil. It must be watered by prayer, nurtured by patience, and tended by humility.

In marriage, love takes root when both individuals are willing to surrender their egos to God's design. It requires learning to love as Christ loved the Church—with sacrifice, compassion, and consistency. The husband's leadership and the wife's partnership are not positions of competition but of covenant harmony. When both are anchored in Christ, neither one must pull the other up or hold the other down. They grow together—stronger, deeper, and more fruitful with time.

Rooted love also understands seasons. Just as every plant experiences cycles of blooming and dormancy, every relationship will have moments of joy and challenge. The couples who thrive are those who remain faithful when the emotions fade and who allow God's Word to nourish their connection. Marriage is not the reward for perfection; it is the classroom of sanctification. Through it, God teaches us patience, humility, and grace. Every disagreement becomes an opportunity to deepen understanding; every reconciliation becomes an act of worship.

When love is rooted in Christ, it also becomes a testimony. Others can sense peace in the way two people treat each other. The world notices marriages that reflect heaven's order—where mutual respect, gentle speech, and steadfast prayer replace pride, harshness, and distance. Love that has taken root doesn't need to be loud; its quiet strength is enough to influence generations.

Sometimes, God allows love to be tested not to destroy it but to deepen it. Conflict, disappointment, and change all expose the quality of the soil in which love was planted. But if both partners return continually to God's Word, forgiveness flows freely, healing takes place, and the roots grow even deeper. "Many waters cannot quench love, nor can the floods drown it" (Song of Solomon 8:7). Divine love endures not because it avoids storms, but because it is anchored in One who calms them.

For singles preparing for marriage, allow love to take root before you reach for the fruit. Become whole before you become one. Let your identity be firm in God so that your relationship will not depend on constant reassurance from another human being. God-designed love is not a rescue mission—it is a partnership of purpose. Two whole people coming together under God's direction create a love that glorifies Him.

For the married, nurture what has been planted. Pray together, listen deeply, and give grace generously. Seasons change, but roots remain. Ask God to help you grow in ways that make your union a reflection of His covenant with the Church—ever faithful, ever forgiving, ever flourishing.

Love that takes root will endure life's winds and weather its storms. It will grow stronger in adversity and more beautiful with time. It will not just survive—it will bear fruit that blesses children, communities, and future generations. Such love is a living witness of God's goodness.

Marriage is not merely the union of two hearts—it is the fusion of two callings under one covenant. It's a garden that must be cultivated with patience, forgiveness, and prayer. The early days may feel effortless, but growth always requires tending.

Love, in its divine form, matures over time. It moves from passion to partnership, from emotion to endurance. True love is less about perfection and more about persistence. 1 Corinthians 13 reminds us that love *"bears all things, believes all things, hopes all things, endures all things."*

Many couples enter marriage expecting constant sunshine, but growth comes through both sunlight and rain. There will be misunderstandings, unmet expectations, and moments of silence—but these are the very spaces where grace grows.

When love takes root in faith, it can withstand any drought. When partners pray together, forgiveness flows more freely. Wholeness in marriage is not found in avoiding conflict but in learning how to grow through it together.

Vignette: The Garden They Rebuilt

Michael and Denise had been married for twenty years when the storms came—financial struggles, misunderstandings, and words spoken in frustration that left silent spaces between them. Counseling helped, but so did something simpler: gardening.

One spring, Denise suggested they rebuild the backyard garden they had abandoned years earlier. Week by week, they cleared the weeds, replanted the soil, and learned to wait again. There were days they said little, but somehow, the work of their hands healed what words could not.

As the first flowers began to bloom, Michael whispered, "It's strange how love is like this garden. It doesn't die—it just needs tending." Denise smiled through tears. "Yes," she said, "and the same God who gave us roots will help us grow again."

By summer, their garden was radiant, and so was their marriage. Their love had taken root again—not because everything was easy, but because they had learned the holy art of watering what still lived.

Reflection: Love as a Living Seed

Every seed must first be buried before it can bloom. In the same way, love must often go through seasons of quiet before it shows its strength. Love is not simply *felt*; it is *formed.* It is in the daily acts of patience, the choice to forgive, and the discipline of kindness that love proves its roots.

Ask yourself: *What kind of soil have I provided for love in my life?* Is it grounded in trust and grace, or tangled in fear and pride? Love cannot thrive where resentment reigns. When we allow God to plow up the hardened ground of our hearts, He creates space for fresh growth.

Love matures when we stop trying to control it and start letting God cultivate it. He is both the Gardener and the Sustainer, tending our hearts until we reflect His image in how we love others.

Life Application: Cultivating Rooted Love

- **Pray for depth, not display.** Ask God to make your love deep enough to withstand difficulty rather than wide enough to impress others.
- **Practice daily nourishment.** Read Scripture together, serve one another, and communicate openly—small acts that feed the roots.
- **Protect the soil.** Guard your relationship from negative voices, old wounds, and unforgiveness that can poison growth.

- **Stay accountable.** Invite mentors, spiritual leaders, or godly friends to speak into your relationship with truth and care.

- **Trust God's timing.** Whether you're waiting for love, rebuilding love, or deepening love, remember that divine timing never disappoints.

When love is rooted in grace, it doesn't just survive seasons—it thrives through them.

Closing Prayer

Heavenly Father,

Thank You for teaching me that true love begins with You. Help me to love from a place of wholeness, not need. For those who are single, let their roots grow deep in Your Word. For the married, strengthen their covenant with grace and understanding. Uproot pride, resentment, and fear, and plant patience, peace, and forgiveness. Let every relationship I am part of reflect Your steadfast love.

In Jesus' name, **Amen.**

Appendix C — Devotional Companion: "When Love Takes Root"

Key Scripture:

"Love suffers long and is kind; love does not envy; love does not parade itself, is not puffed up; does not behave rudely, does not seek its own, is not provoked, thinks no evil; does not rejoice in iniquity, but rejoices in the truth; bears all things, believes all things, hopes all things, endures all things."

— 1 Corinthians 13:4–7 (NKJV)

The Purpose of the Devotional:

To nurture marriages that reflect the covenant heart of God—where love grows deep roots through patience, prayer, and perseverance.

Day 1 — Love as a Choice

Scripture: Colossians 3:14

Reflection: Love is not sustained by emotion but by decision. Feelings may fade, but covenant keeps the promise alive.

Practice: Tell your spouse one reason you still choose them today.

Prayer: *Lord, teach us to love with intention, not just affection.*

Day 2 — The Soil of Communication

Scripture: Proverbs 18:21

Reflection: Words can either water or wither love. Gentle speech softens the heart; harsh words harden it.

Practice: Speak one word of affirmation today that builds instead of critiques.

Prayer: *Father, season our speech with grace so that our words become healing rain to one another.*

Day 3 — Partnership in Prayer

Scripture: Matthew 18:19

Reflection: Couples who pray together invite heaven into their home. Agreement is not just unity of mind—it's unity of spirit.

Practice: Pray with your spouse for five minutes. Ask God to strengthen your unity.

Prayer: *God, make our marriage a sanctuary of prayer and peace.*

Day 4 — Love That Serves

Scripture: Philippians 2:3–4

Reflection: Service in marriage is sacred—it says, "I see you," even when life gets busy.

Practice: Do one act of kindness for your spouse today without mentioning it.

Prayer: *Jesus, teach us to serve each other the way You served us—with humility and joy.*

Day 5 — When Love Needs Healing

Scripture: Ephesians 4:32

Reflection: Every marriage encounters moments of pain. Healing begins where pride ends. Forgiveness is not forgetting; it's releasing.

Practice: Write down one hurt you've carried. Pray together, asking God to heal what has been strained.

Prayer: *Lord, mend what time and words have broken. Teach us to forgive as You forgave us.*

Day 6 — Growing Through Grace

Scripture: 2 Peter 3:18

Reflection: Grace is the secret fertilizer of lasting love. When both partners grow in grace, the marriage blooms again.

Practice: Share one way you've seen your spouse grow since your journey began.

Prayer: *Thank You, Lord, for helping us grow—not perfectly, but faithfully.*

Day 7 — Love That Endures

Scripture: Romans 12:10

Reflection: Mature love doesn't quit when tested; it endures with hope. Every season of marriage—spring, summer, autumn, and winter—teaches love's endurance.

Practice: Renew your vow to love and honor your spouse, even through change.

Prayer: *God, may our love reflect Yours—constant, compassionate, and enduring.*

Love grows the same way trees do: slowly, intentionally, and beneath the surface long before fruit ever appears. In counseling, I often tell couples and individuals that **love cannot thrive where roots are shallow, hearts are crowded, or past wounds remain unhealed**. Healthy love begins with healthy foundations—spiritually, emotionally, and psychologically.

Pastoral Counseling Lens - From the Counseling Chair

This chapter explores what it takes for love to take root and remain rooted through seasons.

1. Attachment Patterns: Love Must Be Planted in Safe Soil

Attachment theory teaches that our earliest relational experiences shape how we love as adults. Many marriages and relationships struggle not because of lack of love, but because:

- The soil of attachment is anxious,
- The soil of self-worth is unstable, or
- The soil of emotional memory is wounded.

A heart with insecure attachment often says:

- "I need you to reassure me constantly."
- "I fear that you will leave me."
- "I expect rejection because it's all I've known."
- "Love feels unsafe, so I protect myself."

But Scripture anchors us in a different reality:

"**Perfect love casts out fear.**" (1 John 4:18 NKJV)

When God heals our attachment wounds:

- fear gives way to faith,
- avoidance gives way to vulnerability,
- self-protection gives way to Christ-centered connection.

Rooted love grows in secure soil.

2. Cognitive Reframing: Rewriting the Story Love Grows From

Many individuals enter relationships with distorted internal narratives such as:

- “I am hard to love.”
- “If people knew the real me, they’d leave.”
- “Love always ends in disappointment.”
- “I must earn affection to keep it.”

These beliefs suffocate relationships before they can bloom.

CBT reframing helps transform these thoughts into truth-filled statements:

- “I am loved by God, and His love makes me worthy.”
- “I can be fully known and still fully accepted.”
- “Past hurt does not define future possibility.”
- “Healthy love is not earned—it is cultivated.”

When the mind is renewed, love gains room to grow. This reframing aligns with Scripture:

“**Be transformed by the renewing of your mind.**” (Romans 12:2)

Healthy love begins with a healthy thought life.

3. Emotional Regulation: Love Requires Steadiness, Not Perfection

Many relationships break down not because of lack of love, but because the partners lack **emotional regulation tools**. When emotions are unmanaged:

- Communication becomes reactive,
- Conflict becomes chaotic,
- Apologies become weapons,
- And silence becomes punishment.

Love that takes root requires:

- Pausing before reacting,
- Listening before defending,
- Praying before responding,
- Regulating rather than exploding.

Emotional regulation is not suppressing emotion; it is stewarding emotion.

Scripture supports this: "**Be angry, and do not sin.**" (Ephesians 4:26)

A regulated heart gives love a stable environment to thrive.

4. Forgiveness Work: Clearing the Soil for New Growth

Unforgiveness is emotional clutter that chokes the roots of intimacy.

Many couples try to build love without first addressing:

- Unspoken resentment
- Old betrayals
- Lingering disappointments
- Childhood wounds
- Past relationship trauma

Jesus teaches that reconciliation isn't optional—it's foundational:

"**Forgive, and you will be forgiven.**" (Luke 6:37)

Forgiveness is not the removal of memory; it is the release of resentment.

Forgiveness prepares the soil for love to flourish.

5. Differentiation: Becoming Whole Enough to Love Well

In pastoral counseling, I often explain **differentiation** as:

"I can love you deeply without losing myself completely."

Love becomes messy when individuals demand from their spouse or partner what only God can provide:

- Identity
- Validation
- Security

- Emotional regulation
- Purpose

When love is rooted in Christ first, it becomes:

- Not clingy, but connected
- Not dependent, but devoted
- Not draining, but nurturing
- Not fearful, but free

Healthy love requires two whole people—not two broken halves.

6. Scriptural Anchoring: Love Rooted in Christ Endures

Every psychological principle in this chapter is reinforced by Scripture:

- **Attachment Security** → "Underneath are the everlasting arms." (Deut. 33:27)

- **Reframing Old Narratives** → "As a man thinks in his heart, so is he." (Prov. 23:7)

- **Emotional Regulation** → "Let every person be swift to hear, slow to speak, slow to anger." (James 1:19)

- **Forgiveness Work** → "Love keeps no record of wrongs." (1 Cor. 13:5)

- **Differentiation & Identity** → "You are complete in Him." (Col. 2:10)

When couples anchor their love in spiritual truth rather than emotional turbulence, roots deepen and fruit appears.

Pastoral Summary

From the counseling chair, **love that takes root is love that has been tended**.

It is:

- Healed from old wounds,
- Grounded in identity,
- Watered by forgiveness,
- Strengthened through prayer,
- And secured in Christ.

Love that grows deep lasts long. Love that is rooted becomes resilient. Love anchored in Christ becomes covenant.

Declaration:

Our love is rooted in Christ. It grows deeper through patience, stronger through prayer, and sweeter through grace. We are partners in purpose—one heart, one covenant, one God.

Closing Benediction for the Week

"And above all things have fervent love for one another, for 'love will cover a multitude of sins.'"— **1 Peter 4:8 (NKJV)**

Chapter 4: Weathering the Heat

"When you pass through the waters, I will be with you; and through the rivers, they shall not overflow you. When you walk through the fire, you shall not be burned, nor shall the flame scorch you."
— **Isaiah 43:2 (NKJV)**

Exegetical Note:

The prophet Isaiah delivers this divine promise to Israel during their exile — a time of collective grief and identity crisis. The Hebrew verb *ʿābar* ("pass through") implies continuity rather than avoidance. God does not promise to keep us from fiery trials but to carry us *through* them.

The phrase *"you shall not be burned"* (*loʾ tiḇʿār*) is both literal and symbolic — expressing divine protection that transcends circumstance. In Scripture, fire often represents testing (*ṣārāp*, "to refine, to purify"). Thus, the text assures that God's presence in adversity does not prevent the flame but transforms its purpose.

Water and fire — symbols of chaos and judgment — become metaphors of purification under divine supervision. God's "witness" becomes the believer's survival.

Historical Context:

Isaiah's audience was facing Babylonian captivity. They had lost their homeland, their temple, and, for many, their hope. Yet God reminds them of His covenant identity: "Fear not, for I have redeemed you; I have called you by your name; you are Mine" (v.1).

These words intentionally echo the Exodus narrative, where Israel crossed the Red Sea (waters) and was guided by a pillar of fire. The God of deliverance was reaffirming His faithfulness in a new generation of bondage.

In both judgment and mercy, God remained constant — shaping His people's endurance through heat and hardship.

Pastoral Insight:

Seasons of heat test the integrity of what's been planted. Pressure reveals what roots conceal. Just as gold is refined by flame, faith matures through trial. The same sun that scorches shallow roots strengthens deep ones.

For believers, "heat" can come as conflict, financial strain, or emotional exhaustion — but the purpose is never destruction. It's transformation. God uses life's furnace to form unshakable trust.

If you find yourself walking through a fiery season, remember: God's presence is the protection. You may feel the warmth of the flame, but you will not be consumed.

You are not burning out; you are being forged.

Even in the warmth of summer, seasons test the soil. Relationships encounter dry spells, communication breaks down, and life applies pressure. But heat doesn't destroy what's deeply rooted—it strengthens it. *"When you pass through the waters, I will be with you; and through the rivers, they shall not overflow you. When you walk through the fire, you shall not be burned"* (Isaiah 43:2 NKJV).

Every lasting relationship will endure seasons of heat—moments that test patience, trust, and humility. The question is not whether challenges will come, but whether we will remain faithful when they do. Faith is not proven on calm days but in the furnace of adversity. When vows are tested, it is faith—not feelings—that holds the covenant together.

Couples who thrive understand that love must be watered daily. Words of encouragement, acts of kindness, and mutual prayer are the irrigation of intimacy. It's not always the storms that destroy marriages—it's the slow drought of neglect. The Song of Solomon warns, "Catch us the foxes, the little foxes that spoil the vines" (Song of Solomon 2:15). The "little foxes" are the small, unaddressed issues that erode trust and intimacy over time.

Even strong marriages can wilt when neglected. But just as the sun can scorch or sustain, heat has a purpose. It draws out impurities, teaches endurance, and deepens dependence on God. When we choose prayer over pride and forgiveness over frustration, the same heat that could have burned us instead refines us. Just as gold is purified in fire, relationships are purified through testing.

There are times when love feels weary—when one partner feels unseen or the other feels unheard. These are the moments when we must remember that marriage was never meant to be maintained by human strength alone. It is a divine covenant that requires divine help. Ecclesiastes reminds us, "A threefold cord is not quickly broken" (Ecclesiastes 4:12). The third strand—God's presence—is what gives marriages their enduring strength.

Seasons of heat also reveal the hidden cracks in the foundation. Pressure doesn't create weakness; it exposes it. Yet exposure is grace, for what is revealed can be healed. God allows relational pressure not to punish but to purify. When we bring our wounds and weariness before Him, He renews the soil of our hearts. The same fire that hardens clay can also forge steel—it depends on what we are made of and Who we allow to shape us.

If you're in a season of relational drought, know that restoration begins not with blame but with surrender. God can breathe life into dry places, but He waits for hearts willing to be refreshed by His presence. Sometimes the greatest miracle is not that your situation changes immediately, but that your spirit does. God can turn indifference into compassion, distance into closeness, and despair into renewed hope.

To weather the heat means learning to pause before reacting, to listen before judging, and to pray before giving up. It means remembering that the same God who was present at the altar is still present in the argument. When you feel the temperature rising, call on the One who calms the storms and cools the heart. "Be still, and know that I am God" (Psalm 46:10).

Just as summer ends with harvest, heated seasons—if endured faithfully—produce fruit. Those who persevere through misunderstanding, financial strain, or health challenges emerge stronger and more united. Their roots go deeper, their faith grows richer, and their love matures beyond surface emotions. The couples who learn to weather the heat often discover that the very trials that once threatened them became the tools that strengthened them.

Vignette: The Couple in the Drought

David and Lena had been married for 15 years when life began to dry up between them. The demands of parenting, work stress, and silent resentment created a distance neither could quite explain. Arguments grew shorter, but so did affection.

One night, after another quiet dinner, Lena whispered, "It feels like we're just surviving." David sighed, "Maybe the well has run dry."

But rather than walk away, they decided to pray together every night for one month, no matter how they felt. At first, the prayers were awkward and brief. Then, as the days passed, something began to shift. The conversations deepened, the silence softened, and tears replaced tension.

One evening, David looked at Lena and said, "Maybe the well wasn't dry—maybe we just stopped drawing water."

The drought ended that night. It wasn't magic; it was mercy. Their love didn't avoid the heat—it was renewed through it. They learned that God doesn't always remove the fire. Sometimes He steps into it with you, just as He did with the three Hebrew boys, and proves that faith still stands firm even in the flames.

Reflection: Finding God in the Heat

Heat reveals what comfort hides. The same trials we wish away are often the very means by which God matures us. When we face pressure, we are forced to depend on grace rather than effort. Spiritual heat exposes pride, impatience, and unspoken pain, but it also ignites endurance and faith.

Ask yourself: *What has the heat revealed in me?*

Have I learned to pray more fervently or to love more gently? God never wastes discomfort. Every heated season has a divine lesson—one that builds character, deepens compassion, and strengthens faith.

When the sun feels too hot, remember: God doesn't send heat to harm you but to harden your faith for what's ahead. What survives the fire comes out stronger, shining with the reflection of His glory.

Life Application: Thriving in Hot Seasons

1. **Stay hydrated spiritually.** Drink deeply from the Word and prayer when life feels dry. Make Scripture your daily refreshment.

2. **Identify your "little foxes."** What small habits or attitudes are spoiling intimacy or joy? Address them before they multiply.

3. **Replace reaction with reflection.** When tensions rise, pause and pray. Ask the Holy Spirit to cool your spirit before you speak.

4. **Invite God into the conversation.** Don't just talk *to* each other—talk *with* God about each other. Shared prayer heals more than shared opinions.

5. **Celebrate survival.** When the heat passes, look back with gratitude. Thank God for what endured and for what was pruned. Faithfulness in heat is the proof of love's depth. Don't despise the fire—it's producing fruit you'll harvest later.

Closing Prayer

Lord God, Thank You for being my shelter in seasons of heat. When the pressures of life and relationships feel overwhelming, remind me that You are near. Teach me to endure with grace, to speak with kindness, and to love with patience. Let the trials that test me refine me instead of breaking me. Breathe new life into every dry place and restore what's been scorched by disappointment. May my faith and my relationships stand firm under Your covering. In Jesus' name, Amen.

Appendix D — Devotional Companion: Weathering the Heat

"When you pass through the waters, I will be with you; and through the rivers, they shall not overflow you. When you walk through the fire, you

shall not be burned, nor shall the flame scorch you."— **Isaiah 43:2 (NKJV)**

Purpose of This Devotional

Heat tests, but it also purifies. Each day will remind you that adversity doesn't destroy faith—it deepens it. The God who walks with you through fire also brings forth gold from your endurance.

Day 1 — Faith Under Fire

Scripture: Daniel 3:25

Reflection: God doesn't always take the heat away—He steps into it with you.

Practice: Write down one "fire" you are facing and one way you've seen God's presence within it

Prayer: *Lord, thank You for standing with me in the flames. Strengthen my faith until the smoke clears.*

Day 2 — Pressure Produces Purpose

Scripture: 2 Corinthians 4:8–9

Reflection: Pressure doesn't prove weakness; it reveals what's inside. Your endurance is producing glory.

Practice: Reflect on a past season of pressure. What fruit did it eventually bear?

Prayer: *Father, transform my pressure into purpose and my trial into testimony.*

Day 3 — The Purpose of Testing

Scripture: James 1:2–4

Reflection: Tests are not punishments; they are promotions in disguise. God refines faith the way fire refines gold.

Practice: List one lesson your current challenge is teaching you

Prayer: *God, use my trials to strengthen my trust in You.*

Day 4 — Staying Cool in Conflict

Scripture: Proverbs 15:1

Reflection: Heat often shows up in relationships. A soft answer is a cooling balm to burning emotions.

Practice: When tension rises, respond with calm instead of reaction.

Prayer: *Holy Spirit, guard my words so peace prevails over pride.*

Day 5 — The Restoration of Rain

Scripture: Hosea 6:3

Reflection: After every dry spell comes refreshing rain. God has not forgotten your field.

Practice: Step outside today and breathe deeply. Thank God for renewal that follows every drought.

Prayer: *Lord, send Your rain of refreshing over every weary place in my life.*

Day 6 — The Heat That Heals

Scripture: Malachi 3:3

Reflection: God is like a refiner's fire—not to consume, but to cleanse. His heat removes impurities that hinder holiness.

Practice: Ask God to show you one attitude or habit He's refining right now.

Prayer: *Purify my motives, Lord. Let the fire of Your Spirit make me more like You.*

Day 7 — Endurance That Shines

Scripture: Romans 5:3–5

Reflection: Endurance produces character, and character hope. The fire that tested you will soon testify for you.

Practice: Write a short praise note about how God has sustained you through a recent trial.

Prayer: *Thank You, Lord, for turning my trials into triumphs and my pain into praise.*

Every relationship faces seasons of heat—moments when pressure intensifies, patience wears thin, and communication dries up. From the counseling chair, I have seen this truth repeatedly: **heat doesn't destroy healthy relationships; it reveals their strength.** And where strength is lacking, heat exposes where healing must begin.

This chapter speaks to the emotional, psychological, and spiritual tools needed to withstand relational droughts, misunderstandings, and seasons of internal or external pressure.

Pastoral Counseling Lens - From the Counseling Chair

Emotional Regulation Under Pressure: Responding, Not Reacting

Heat often manifests as conflict, tension, miscommunication, or emotional overwhelm. When pressure rises, people tend to react from instinct rather than intention:

- Withdrawing,
- Shutting down,
- Escalating anger,
- Over-explaining,
- Blaming, or
- Becoming defensive.

Emotional regulation becomes the cooling system of the heart.

Scripture anchors this truth:

"A soft answer turns away wrath, but a harsh word stirs up anger." (Proverbs 15:1)

In counseling, I teach three stabilizing practices:

- **Pause** — Take emotional inventory before speaking.

- **Process** — Name the emotion behind the reaction (hurt? fear? disappointment?)

- **Pray** — Invite the Holy Spirit into the moment before responding.

Couples who learn these rhythms reduce conflict by 50–70%, not because heat disappears but because their hearts stay regulated.

Cognitive Reframing: Pressure Is Not Punishment

When stress hits, many individuals interpret pressure as personal failure or relational doom:

- “We’re arguing—something is wrong with us.”
- “If it’s difficult, it must not be God’s will.”
- “Maybe we’re not compatible.”
- “This is too hard—why even try?”

But Scripture reframes heat as refinement, not destruction:

“**When you walk through the fire… you shall not be burned.**” (Isaiah 43:2)

CBT reframing helps reshape these thoughts:

Old Thought: “This pressure is breaking us.”

Reframed Truth: “This pressure is showing us where to grow.”

Old Thought: “We keep having conflict—something’s wrong.”

Reframed Truth: “Conflict is a doorway to deeper understanding.”

Old Thought: “If love was real, it wouldn’t be this hard.”

Reframed Truth: "Deep love requires deep work."

Heat sanctifies. It clarifies. It strengthens. And it always reveals what God desires to heal.

Attachment Dynamics in Heated Seasons

Attachment patterns become most visible during conflict.

The anxiously attached partner may become:

- Clingy
- Hyper-vigilant
- Emotionally flooded
- Fearful of abandonment

The Avoidantly attached partner may:

- Shut down
- Withdraw
- Minimize emotions
- Appear indifferent

Both are reacting from childhood roots, not present realities.

Through pastoral counseling, I gently guide individuals to see that **their partner's heat response often reflects an old wound, not a new offense**.

The gospel meets both attachments:

- To the anxious heart → "I will never leave you." (Hebrews 13:5)
- To the avoidant heart → "Cast your cares…" (1 Peter 5:7)

Rooted love grows when partners learn to respond to each other's wounds rather than react to each other's words.

Forgiveness & Repair: Watering Love in a Dry Season

Heat dries out the soil of intimacy unless relationships practice repair.

Forgiveness during heated seasons is not merely saying "I forgive you," but choosing to:

- Soften your tone,
- Revisit conflict after emotions settle,
- Apologize without excuses,
- Validate the other person's experience,
- Ask "how can we do better next time?"

Jesus modeled repair long before psychology named it:

"**Blessed are the peacemakers…**" (Matthew 5:9)

Forgiveness is the water that keeps hearts from cracking open under heat.

Resilience Building: Heat Creates Stronger Roots

From a therapeutic perspective, resilience is the ability to withstand difficulty without losing identity, emotional balance, or hope.

Spiritually, resilience is faith under fire.

Heat often creates:

- Stronger communication skills,
- Deeper appreciation,
- Renewed commitment,
- Clearer boundaries,
- Healthier expectations,
- And a more Christ-centered partnership.

What feels like relational fire becomes relational formation.

"**Tribulation produces perseverance; perseverance, character; and character, hope.**" (Romans 5:3–4)

Heat is never wasted in the life of the believer. It is a divine strengthening season.

Scriptural Anchoring: The God Who Stands in the Fire

Every counseling principle in this chapter finds its foundation in Scripture:

- **Emotional Regulation** → "Be slow to speak, slow to wrath." (James 1:19)

- **Reframing Stress** → "Count it all joy…" (James 1:2–4)

- **Attachment Healing** → "The Lord is near…" (Psalm 34:18)

- **Forgiveness & Repair** → "Bear with one another… forgive." (Colossians 3:13)

- **Resilience** → "You shall not be burned." (Isaiah 43:2)
  The fourth man still walks in the fire (Daniel 3). This means no believer weathering relational heat is ever alone.

Pastoral Summary

From the counseling chair, I see heat not as a threat, but as an indicator.

Heat reveals:

- What needs healing,
- Where communication must improve,
- What childhood wounds resurface under pressure,
- Where emotional regulation needs strengthening,
- And how deeply rooted the relationship truly is.

Heat invites couples and individuals to grow—not apart, but deeper.

When handled with grace, patience, and prayer, heated seasons produce not destruction, but **refinement**.

Love that survives the heat emerges stronger, wiser, humbler, and more anchored in Christ.

Declaration:

I am refined, not ruined. God's fire makes me faithful, not fearful. I am coming forth as gold—purified, patient, and prepared for greater purpose.

Closing Benediction for the Week

"But He knows the way that I take; when He has tested me, I shall come forth as gold."— **Job 23:10 (NKJV)**

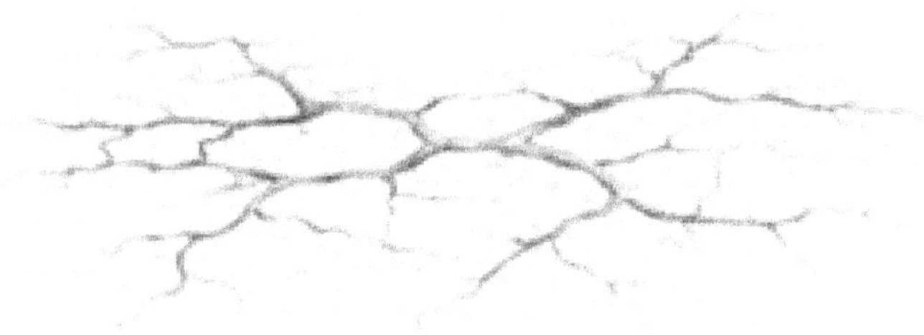

Part 2: The Autumn and Winter Seasons

Autumn *is the season of* release. *It is the holy letting go of what has served its purpose. The falling leaves remind us that surrender is not loss—it is trust in motion. Autumn says, "Yield." It invites us to shed resentment, pride, and fear so that our hearts might breathe again. It's in letting go that we make room for what's next.*

Winter *speaks of* restoration. *It is the quiet, still season when God hides us to heal us. Beneath the stillness, He is preparing new life. Winter says, "Rest." It calls us to silence our striving and to rediscover peace in His presence. Though the landscape may seem barren, the promise of renewal lies just beneath the frost.*

Part 2

The Autumn and
Winter Seasons

Chapter 5: The Grace to Let Go

"Casting all your care upon Him, for He cares for you."
— 1 Peter 5:7 (NKJV)

Exegetical Note:

The word *"casting"* comes from the Greek verb ***epiripsantes*** — meaning "to intentionally throw upon, to release with force, to place decisively." It is not a gentle suggestion but an act of surrender. Peter uses the same verb found in Luke 19:35, when the disciples *threw* their cloaks upon the colt for Jesus to ride — a deliberate transfer of weight.

The word *"care"* (*merimna*) means "anxiety produced by dividing the mind." Worry fractures the inner world. Letting go, therefore, is not weakness—it is spiritual wholeness.

Peter's phrase *"for He cares for you"* is written in the present active tense, meaning:

God is continuously, actively, attentively caring for you. Letting go is not an act of abandonment; it is an act of placement — putting your grief, fear, or disappointment into God's capable hands.

Historical Context:

Peter wrote this letter to believers suffering under systemic oppression, social displacement, and rising persecution under Emperor Nero. They were exhausted, misunderstood, and grieving the loss of normalcy. The temptation was to carry emotional burdens silently.

Peter, once the disciple who tried to fix everything himself, now writes as a shepherd softened by grace. He encourages the suffering church to do spiritually what he had learned to do personally—release control. His command to "cast your cares" is not naïve optimism but pastoral wisdom forged through failure, restoration, and surrender.

He reminds them—and us—that God's care is not theoretical. It is present, personal, and protective.

Pastoral Insight:

Letting go is often the hardest obedience, because it requires trusting God with incomplete closure. Releasing what hurt you, who left you, or what ended feels like stepping into uncertainty. Yet Scripture reveals that release is the doorway to rest.

God cannot fill hands that refuse to open.

He cannot heal what we insist on holding.

He cannot restore what we refuse to release.

Letting go is not giving up — it is giving God room.

It's the spiritual courage to say: **"Lord, I trust You with what I cannot change."**

Autumn leaves fall not because the tree is dying, but because the tree is preparing for new life.

So, it is with you.

What you release in faith, God receives in love.

There is a sacred kind of strength that comes from surrender. We often think grace is what carries us through holding on, but sometimes grace is what empowers us to release. Autumn reminds us that even beautiful things must fall so that new life can grow. What once provided shade in one season must sometimes be released in another.

Letting go is not failure—it is faith in motion. When we loosen our grip on what has ended, we open our hearts to what God still desires to begin. "Casting all your care upon Him, for He cares for you" (1 Peter 5:7 NKJV). There is something liberating about releasing what you were never meant to carry. The weight that once felt noble becomes unbearable when it no longer aligns with God's purpose.

In counseling, I've met people who grieve not only what they lost but also what they thought life would be—the dream that ended, the marriage that changed, the expectation that never materialized. Yet grief is the soil where grace grows. Jesus said, "Blessed are those who mourn, for they shall be comforted" (Matthew 5:4 NKJV). Grief, when surrendered to God, becomes a pathway to peace. It reminds us that endings are not punishments; they are transitions to something new.

When life invites us into an autumn season, God asks us to release the leaves that no longer serve us—bitterness, resentment, self-blame, and even the illusion of control. Just as trees must shed their covering to survive winter, we too must let go of the weight that keeps us from growing. Letting go is not the same as giving up. Giving up says, "It's over." Letting go says, "God, I trust You with what's next." It is a holy exchange—our burden for His peace.

Letting go requires courage because it calls us to face the unknown. Faith steps into the spaces that fear avoids. Abraham left everything familiar because God whispered a promise greater than his comfort (Genesis 12:1-2). His obedience teaches us that sometimes, you cannot receive the blessing until you release the familiar. God's grace will not fail you when He calls you to release what no longer fits the destiny He has for you.

In relationships, letting go can mean accepting that reconciliation may not look like restoration. Sometimes God closes a chapter not to hurt you, but to heal you. Holding on to someone or something that no longer bears fruit can drain the spiritual life from your soul. Even Jesus told His disciples, "If they do not receive you, shake off the dust from your feet" (Matthew 10:14). There is grace in shaking off what hinders peace.

Letting go may also mean releasing your own mistakes—laying down the guilt of what you could not fix or the shame of what you did not foresee. God's forgiveness is not partial; it is complete. "As far as the east is from the west, so far has He removed our transgressions from us" (Psalm 103:12). When you forgive yourself, you make space for God's restoration to begin. You stop rehearsing what you can't change and start receiving what He's redeeming.

The grace to let go is also the grace to grow. God prunes not to punish but to make room for new fruit. "Every branch that bears fruit He prunes, that it may bear more fruit" (John 15:2). The pruning is painful, but it is purposeful. What falls away is not meant to define you; it is meant to refine you. When you learn to let go without bitterness, you become lighter, freer, and more aligned with God's next assignment for your life.

Autumn is both a release and a renewal. It is the sound of leaves falling and the whisper of God saying, "I'm still here." The trees don't fear losing what they've carried—they trust the One who designed the seasons. Likewise, when you release what has served its season, you make room for the harvest that follows surrender. You discover that peace is not found in control but in trust.

Letting go does not mean you stop caring—it means you start healing. It means you allow God to write the next line of your story without trying to edit the last one. It's choosing faith over fear, release over regret, and surrender over striving. The grace to let go is God's invitation to breathe again.

Vignette: The Box by the Door

Tanya had been divorced for two years but couldn't bring herself to clear the last box of her former husband's belongings from the hallway closet. It wasn't the box itself—it was what it represented: dreams, identity, and years that couldn't be reclaimed.

One morning, after prayer, she sensed God whisper, *"It's time."* She carried the box to the door, tears streaming, and said aloud, "Lord, I release what was and receive what will be." It wasn't dramatic—no music, no audience—but heaven witnessed her obedience.

That afternoon, she noticed sunlight streaming through the window in a way she hadn't seen before. The space the box once occupied seemed brighter. Tanya smiled and said softly, "So this is what freedom feels like."

Sometimes letting go is as simple as making room for light again.

Reflection: The Freedom in Falling Leaves

Every leaf that falls is an act of trust. The tree releases what no longer nourishes it because it knows the cycle of life is not ending—it's transforming. In your life, there are habits, relationships, and expectations that have completed their purpose. Holding on will only exhaust you.

Letting go is a spiritual decision to believe that God is not finished, even if a chapter is. He can bring new beauty to barren branches. Release is not loss—it's preparation for resurrection.

Ask yourself: *What am I still holding that God has already healed?* Sometimes the miracle begins not when something new starts, but when you finally stop resisting what must end.

Life Application: Practicing the Grace of Release

1. **Name what you must release.** Write it down and pray over it. Clarity breaks the emotional tie that keeps you bound.

2. **Replace bitterness with blessing.** Each time the memory returns, speak a word of thanksgiving for what you learned.

3. **Re-center your worth.** Remind yourself: "My value is not attached to what I lost but to the One who loves me."

4. **Rest instead of wrestle.** Spend intentional time in stillness—silence is the soil of surrender.

5. **Rebuild with purpose.** After release, ask, "Lord, what are You preparing me for now?" God never asks you to let go without giving you something better to hold.

Grace begins where grasping ends.

Closing Prayer

Loving Father,

Thank You for the strength that comes through surrender. Teach me to release what no longer serves Your purpose and to trust You with what's ahead. Help me to let go without bitterness and to rest in Your perfect timing. Heal the parts of my heart that still cling to what You've already called complete. I receive Your peace, your restoration, and Your grace to move forward in faith.

In Jesus' name, Amen.

Appendix E — Devotional Companion: The Grace to Let Go

Key Scripture: *"Casting all your care upon Him, for He cares for you."*— **1 Peter 5:7 (NKJV)**

The Purpose of the Devotional: Letting go is not giving up—it's growing up. These reflections help the reader release what has ended and make space for what God is beginning.

Day 1 — The Sacred Release

Scripture: Ecclesiastes 3:6

Reflection: Every ending has divine purpose. Releasing is a form of trust—saying, "God, you know what to keep and what to remove."

Practice: Write down one thing you're still trying to control and pray over it.

Prayer: *Lord, teach me to release what's Yours to handle and rest in Your peace.*

Day 2 — Freedom in Forgiveness

Scripture: Matthew 6:14–15

Reflection: Forgiveness unties the knots that keep us bound to old pain. It doesn't excuse the wrong; it releases its power.

Practice: Name one person or moment that still weighs on you. Choose to forgive today.

Prayer: *Father, help me to forgive as You've forgiven me—completely and freely.*

Day 3 — When Holding on Hurts

Scripture: Hebrews 12:1

Reflection: Carrying yesterday's burdens blocks tomorrow's blessings. God can't fill hands that are already full.

Practice: Symbolically open your hands as you pray, releasing the weight of what you can't change.

Prayer: *Lord, loosen my grip on what drains my spirit. Make room for Your renewing grace.*

Day 4 — Grieving with Grace

Scripture: Psalm 30:5

Reflection: Grief is not a lack of faith; it's love seeking expression. Let tears become worship.

Practice: Write a gratitude letter to God for what that season taught you.

Prayer: *God, thank You for the beauty hidden even in my tears. Turn my mourning into dancing again.*

Day 5 — Releasing Regret

Scripture: Isaiah 43:18–19

Reflection: You can't drive forward by staring in the rearview mirror. God is doing a new thing—don't miss it by looking back.

Practice: List your biggest "if only," then declare aloud, "God has forgiven me, and I forgive myself."

Prayer: *Thank You, Lord, for freeing me from yesterday's shadows so I can walk in today's light.*

Day 6 — Making Room for Renewal

Scripture: John 15:2

Reflection: Pruning is painful but necessary. God removes what limits your fruitfulness so that growth can flourish.

Practice: Clear one physical space in your home as a symbolic act of spiritual decluttering.

Prayer: *Father, prune me with purpose. Remove what hinders and restore what heals.*

Day 7 — Trusting the Unknown

Scripture: Proverbs 3:5–6

Reflection: Faith flourishes in the unknown. Letting go isn't losing control—it's handing control back to God.

Practice: Pray for courage to embrace uncertainty with confidence in His plan.

Prayer: *Lord, I trust you even when I cannot trace You. Order my steps and settle my soul.*

Pastoral Counseling Lens - From the Counseling Chair

Letting go is one of the most difficult emotional and spiritual processes a believer faces. In pastoral counseling, I have witnessed people wrestle not only with what they lost, but with the *meaning* they attached to the loss. Much of the pain of releasing comes from the stories we tell ourselves about what the loss says about us.

Yet Scripture shows that letting go is not abandonment—it is alignment with God's movement. And therapeutically, release is a vital part of emotional health, identity recovery, and spiritual restoration.

1. Cognitive Reframing: Release as a Form of Trust, Not Failure

People often interpret letting go as:

- "I failed."
- "I should have tried harder."
- "If I were stronger, this wouldn't have happened."
- "I'm losing something I need to be whole."

But Scripture reframes letting go as a holy act:

"**Casting all your care upon Him…**" (1 Peter 5:7)

"**Forget the former things… behold, I will do a new thing.**" (Isaiah 43:18–19)

Therapeutic Reframe:

Letting go is not giving up—it is giving God room to work.

Instead of "I'm losing everything," the truth becomes: *"I'm letting go so God can lead me into what's next."*

Instead of "This ended because I'm unworthy," the truth becomes: *"This ended because God is redirecting my story."*

Instead of "I'll never recover," the truth becomes: *"Healing is possible, and God is with me in the process."*

Reframing helps individuals release shame while embracing new beginnings.

2. Grief Work: Honoring What Was Without Clinging to It

Letting go always involves grief—whether the loss is:

- A relationship,
- A dream,
- A season of life,
- A sense of identity,
- Or a hope that never came to pass.

In counseling, I help individuals understand that grief is not weakness—it is witness.

Jesus said, "**Blessed are those who mourn…**" (Matthew 5:4)

Healthy grief work includes:

- Naming the loss
- Honoring what was good
- Acknowledging what was painful
- Allowing emotions to surface without judgment
- Accepting that mourning is part of healing

When people allow God into their grief, the soil of release becomes fertile ground for restoration.

3. Attachment Healing: Untangling Identity from What Ended

Many people struggle to let go because what they lost became intertwined with who they believed they were.

Attachment healing explores:

- What did this season or relationship represent?
- What identity did it give me?
- What fear rises when I imagine life without it?
- What need was I expecting it to fill?

Letting go requires separating **identity from attachment**.

Scripture anchors this truth:

"You are complete in Him." (Colossians 2:10)

When a believer learns that:

- Purpose is not tied to people,
- Identity is not tied to seasons, and
- Wholeness is not tied to relationships—letting go becomes liberation, not devastation.

4. Emotional Regulation: Managing the Turbulence of Release

Letting go can trigger emotional waves:

- Anxiety
- Sadness
- Rumination
- Regret
- Fear of the unknown
- Longing for closure

Emotional regulation helps individuals navigate these emotions without being overtaken by them.

Effective practices include:

- Breath prayer ("Lord, calm my heart.")
- Journaling the release process
- Practicing grounding techniques
- Speaking Scripture aloud
- Identifying emotional triggers
- Replacing "What if…" thoughts with "Even if… God is with me."

Release is not an overnight event—it is a regulated journey.

1. Forgiveness Work: Clearing Bitterness to Make Room for Newness

Letting go often requires forgiveness:

- Forgiving yourself,
- Forgiving someone else,
- Or forgiving a season that disappointed you.

Forgiveness clears the emotional residue that keeps a person tied to what God is trying to move them beyond.

"**Forgive as Christ forgave you.**" (Colossians 3:13)

Forgiveness is not

- Reconciliation.
- Forgetting.
- Endorsing the pain.

Forgiveness is the spiritual act that untangles your heart from the past so your future can begin.

Behavioral Activation: Small Steps Toward a New Season

One of the biggest counseling breakthroughs occurs when individuals take small, intentional steps that signal to the brain:

"I am moving forward."

These steps may include:

- Redecorating a room
- Starting a new routine
- Returning to a hobby
- Connecting with supportive community
- Setting new boundaries
- Practicing self-care without guilt

These actions reinforce the emotional truth of release.

Faith without works is dead—and healing without movement stalls.

1. Scriptural Anchoring: Release Is Sacred, Not Shameful

Every therapeutic principle in this chapter is reflected in Scripture:

- **Reframing Loss** → "He makes all things new." (Rev. 21:5)

- **Grief Work** → "Those who sow in tears shall reap in joy." (Psalm 126:5)

- **Attachment Healing** → "Underneath are the everlasting arms." (Deut. 33:27)

- **Emotional Regulation** → "Be anxious for nothing…" (Phil. 4:6–7)

- **Forgiveness Work** → "Love keeps no record of wrongs." (1 Cor. 13:5)

- **Moving Forward** → "Arise… for this is your season." (Isaiah 60:1)
  Release is a spiritual discipline of trust.

Pastoral Summary

From the counseling chair, I see letting go as a holy act of cooperation with God. It is:

- The unclenching of the hands,
- The quiet surrender of the heart,
- The releasing of what cannot remain,
- The acceptance of what god is preparing,
- And the trust that new life is on the horizon.

Letting go is grace in motion.

When you release what God has removed, you make room for what God desires to restore.

Declaration

I release what was and receive what will be. I am no longer bound by bitterness but freed by faith. The grace to let go has made room for God to restore me fully.

Closing Benediction for the Week

"Blessed are those who mourn, for they shall be comforted." — Matthew 5:4 (NKJV

Chapter 6: The Beauty of Brokenness

"The Lord is near to those who have a broken heart, and saves such as have a contrite spirit."— **Psalm 34:18 (NKJV)**

Exegetical Note:

The Hebrew word for *"broken"* here is ***shābar*** — meaning *"to break in pieces, to crush, to fracture beyond one's own ability to repair."* It describes more than sadness; it describes a soul shattered by loss, betrayal, disappointment, or regret.

Yet the verb for *"near"* (**qārôb**) implies not simple proximity, but *intentional closeness* — God steps toward the brokenhearted with deliberate nearness.

The word *"contrite"* comes from ***dākkā'*** — meaning *"crushed to powder, humbled to dust."* In Scripture, contrition is not humiliation; it is holy surrender — the posture that invites divine restoration.

The verse does not say God fixes all circumstances first. It says He *saves* the crushed *spirit* first. Brokenness, therefore, is not a disqualification — it is an invitation.

Historical Context:

David penned this psalm during one of the lowest moments of his life. Fleeing from King Saul, he sought refuge among the Philistines and pretended madness to survive (1 Samuel 21). He had lost reputation, stability, and security. He was anointed for a throne he could not touch, living in caves instead of palaces.

This psalm was birthed from a man who knew the heartbreak of disappointment, fear, and isolation — yet also the intimacy of God's nearness in the darkest places.

David discovered that brokenness did not drive God away; it drew God in.

Pastoral Insight:

Brokenness is often the birthplace of revelation. It is where God shows us not what we can do for Him, but what He does in us.

We try to avoid breaking, but God often uses the breaking to reveal the beauty. The world sees brokenness as failure. God sees it as fertile ground for transformation.

In God's hands:

- Broken hearts become open hearts.
- Broken dreams become redirected destinies.
- Broken seasons become sacred chapters.

You are not too shattered to be used. You are not too wounded to be whole. You are not too broken for God to draw near.

Brokenness is not the end — it's the beginning of becoming.

Your broken places are the very spaces where God's glory gets in.

Brokenness is not the end of your story—it's the birthplace of your ministry. Some of the most powerful testimonies are born out of the cracks we tried to hide. "The Lord is near to those who have a broken heart, and saves such as have a contrite spirit" (Psalm 34:18 NKJV).

We live in a world that fears pain, but God uses it as a teacher. When we are broken, we discover the God who binds up wounds. It is through tears that we learn tenderness, and through sorrow that we gain empathy for others. The moments that feel like endings are often God's way of preparing us for a greater beginning. Brokenness becomes sacred when we allow God to transform it into purpose.

I once counseled a man who said, "I feel like I'm falling apart." My response was gentle but firm: "Maybe you're not falling apart—maybe you're falling into God." Brokenness draws us to dependency. It humbles us, purifies us, and positions us for His power. When we no longer have the strength to stand on our own, we finally learn how to lean on Him.

Consider David's cry: "Create in me a clean heart, O God, and renew a steadfast spirit within me" (Psalm 51:10 NKJV). David's restoration didn't come through perfection—it came through repentance. He discovered that brokenness can be holy when it drives us back to the feet of God. The same God who anointed him as king also forgave him as sinner. God doesn't discard the broken; He redesigns them.

If you are walking through a broken season, remember that even Jesus chose to show His scars after resurrection. Your healing will not erase your history—it will redeem it. Your scars become your sermon. They tell the world, "I've been through the fire, but I'm still here." The resurrection didn't erase the wounds in Jesus' hands; it revealed that what once was pain had become proof of victory.

Brokenness is not the absence of strength—it is the doorway to it. Every fracture becomes a place where God's light can shine through. The Japanese art of *kintsugi*—the repairing of broken pottery with gold—teaches that what is mended becomes more valuable than before. Likewise, God's grace fills the cracks of our lives with His glory until our story gleams with redemption.

Pain has a way of stripping away pretense. When we are broken, titles and positions no longer matter—only presence does. In those moments, we stop performing for God and start resting in Him. It is there that intimacy is renewed. The same God who sits high is the One who kneels beside us in the ashes, whispering, "You are still Mine."

Every broken place has a lesson. Broken trust teaches discernment. Broken dreams awaken new vision. Broken relationships deepen compassion. God never wastes what breaks us. When we yield our pain to Him, He reshapes it into wisdom that blesses others. "We comfort those in any trouble with the comfort we ourselves receive from God" (2 Corinthians 1:4). Your healing becomes someone else's hope.

The journey of brokenness is not linear. There will be days of progress and days of pain, but both are part of the process. God never rushes healing because He cares more about wholeness than speed. The Potter does not throw away clay that cracks under pressure; He adds water, reshapes it, and molds it again. What feels like starting over is often God's way of creating something better than before.

If your heart is aching, take comfort in knowing that God sees the tears no one else does. He collects them, redeems them, and waters your next season with them. Brokenness is not your identity—it is your testimony in progress. You will emerge not as you were, but as who you were meant to be all along: whole, restored, and radiant in grace.

Vignette: The Potter's Table

Cynthia had spent years feeling like a failure after her divorce. She often said, "I'm just too broken to be used." One afternoon, her friend invited her to a pottery class. Reluctantly, she went.

The instructor demonstrated how a cracked vase could be repaired using a Japanese method called *kintsugi*—where broken pottery is mended with gold, making it more beautiful for having been broken. Cynthia watched in awe as the golden seams shimmered in the light.

The instructor smiled and said, "We don't hide the cracks. We highlight them. They tell the story of endurance."

That evening, Cynthia prayed differently. "Lord," she whispered, "thank You for my golden seams." From that day forward, she began mentoring other women who had experienced heartbreak. Her ministry was born not from perfection, but from restoration.

Her brokenness had not ended her story—it had refined her calling.

Reflection: The Gift Hidden in the Fracture

There is a quiet holiness in brokenness—a sacred invitation to meet God in the fragments. We often try to glue our lives back together before allowing Him to heal us from within. But true healing doesn't come from reassembly; it comes from restoration.

Ask yourself: *What if my brokenness is not a curse but a calling?* God uses the things that wounded us to equip us for ministry. The same hands that once trembled in grief can now lift others in grace. Every fracture that was surrendered has the potential to become a window for God's light.

When you let go of the need to appear unbroken, you become a vessel of authenticity through which others can see Christ's love clearly.

Life Application: Living Whole Through What Broke You

1. **Stop hiding the cracks.** Share your story. Someone else's healing may be waiting for your honesty.

2. **Shift your language.** Instead of saying, "I'm broken," begin to say, "I'm being rebuilt."

3. **Let the Word wash the wounds.** Read and pray through Psalm 34, Isaiah 61, and 2 Corinthians 4 until they take root in your heart.

4. **Redefine strength.** Real strength is not the absence of pain but the ability to praise God through it.

5. **Serve from your scars.** Find a way to bless others through the lessons your pain taught you—teach, write, mentor, or simply listen.

Brokenness in God's hands becomes a bridge for others to find hope.

Closing Prayer

Heavenly Father, Thank You for meeting me in my broken places. When I feel shattered, remind me that You are the Potter and I am the clay. Use every scar, every wound, and every tear for Your glory. Let my story bring healing to others who are hurting. Teach me to see beauty where I once saw brokenness, and peace where I once saw pain. Make me whole again—not flawless, but faithful. In Jesus' name, Amen.

Appendix F — Devotional Companion: Beauty from Brokenness

Key Scripture: *"The Lord is near to those who have a broken heart, and saves such as have a contrite spirit."*— **Psalm 34:18 (NKJV)**

Purpose of this Devotional: Brokenness is not the end of your story—it's the doorway to deeper intimacy with God. This devotional companion invites reflection on how He brings beauty out of what we thought was beyond repair.

Day 1 — The God Who Stays Near

Scripture: Psalm 147:3

Reflection: God does not avoid your pain; He abides in it. His nearness is the first step of healing.

Practice: Sit in silence for five minutes today and simply acknowledge His presence.

Prayer: *Lord, thank You for drawing close to my broken heart. Let Your nearness be my comfort.*

Day 2 — Embracing the Fragments

Scripture: John 6:12

Reflection: Jesus told His disciples to gather the fragments so that nothing would be lost. God does the same with us—He collects every piece.

Practice: Write down one "fragment" of your past that God is redeeming.

Prayer: *Father, gather the broken pieces of my story and use them to feed others with hope.*

Day 3 — The Gift of Vulnerability

Scripture: 2 Corinthians 12:9

Reflection: Weakness is not failure; it is a frame for grace. When we are transparent, God's strength becomes visible.

Practice: Share your story with someone who needs encouragement today.

Prayer: *Lord, let my transparency become a testimony of Your power.*

Day 4 — Healing in the Light

Scripture: 1 John 1:7

Reflection: Hiding prolongs pain. Healing begins in honesty. When light touches the wound, restoration begins.

Practice: Journal one area you've been afraid to bring into the light. Offer it to God.

Prayer: *Jesus, shine Your light on the hidden parts of my heart. Heal me from the inside out.*

Day 5 — When the Pieces Don't Fit Yet

Scripture: Romans 8:28

Reflection: God sees the full picture while we only see the puzzle. What feels misplaced today will reveal its purpose tomorrow.

Practice: Write: "God is still working." Place it where you can see it this week.

Prayer: *Lord, I trust you with the unfinished parts of my life. You make all things beautiful in time.*

Day 6 — The Ministry of Scars

Scripture: John 20:27

Reflection: Even Jesus chose to show His scars. Your healing will not erase your story—it will empower it.

Practice: Reflect on one past hurt that now equips you to help others.

Prayer: *Father, thank You that my scars no longer symbolize shame, but survival and grace.*

Day 7 — Beauty from the Ashes

Scripture: Isaiah 61:3

Reflection: God never wastes pain. The ashes of brokenness become soil for beauty, strength, and new beginnings.

Practice: Write a prayer of thanksgiving for how far you've come.

Prayer: *Lord, thank You for turning my mourning into mission and my pain into praise.*

Pastoral Counseling Lens - From the Counseling Chair

Brokenness is a word many fears, but in Nouthetic counseling, I have learned that **brokenness is often the birthplace of breakthrough**. When individuals enter my counseling room feeling shattered, I gently remind them that God does His best work with broken pieces. What looks like the end is often the beginning of a deeper, truer, more Spirit-led wholeness.

This chapter reflects the therapeutic and spiritual truth that God does not waste pain—He transforms it.

1. Trauma-Informed Care: Naming the Wound Without Becoming It

Many people confuse brokenness with identity. Trauma has a way of whispering:

- "You are the mistake."
- "You are unworthy."
- "You are too damaged to be loved."

- "Your story ends here."

But trauma-informed counseling teaches that while pain shapes us, it does *not* define us.

Scripture supports this truth:

"The Lord is near to the brokenhearted." (Psalm 34:18)

In therapy, the first step is **naming the wound**, not wearing it.

Healing begins when individuals say:

- "This happened *to* me, but it is not who I am."
- "My pain is real, but so is God's plan."
- "I can be wounded and still be worthy."

Brokenness becomes breakthrough when identity shifts from *the event* to *the Redeemer*.

2. Cognitive Processing: Rewriting the Story the Pain Told

One of the most powerful counseling tools is helping individuals examine the internal narratives formed in seasons of pain.

Cognitive processing asks:

- What meaning did I attach to this suffering?
- What lie did my pain teach me?

- What truth does God speak instead?

Old Narrative: "This loss ruined me."

Breakthrough Narrative: "This loss refined me."

Old Narrative: "I am broken beyond repair."

Breakthrough Narrative: "I am broken open for God to rebuild."

Old Narrative: "My struggles disqualify me."

Breakthrough Narrative: "My struggles prepare me."

This reframing aligns with Scripture: "

Behold, I am making all things new." (Revelation 21:5)

Brokenness becomes breakthrough when the mind is renewed.

3. Somatic Awareness: Listening to What the Body Has Been Holding

Brokenness doesn't stay in the mind—it settles in the body.

• Tight shoulders• Shallow breathing• Knots in the stomach• Restlessness• Fatigue• Chronic tension

In counseling, somatic (body-centered) awareness helps individuals reconnect with the physical manifestations of emotional pain.

David's lament in Psalm 32 reflects this truth: "**My bones grew old… my vitality was turned into drought.**"

Breakthrough comes when individuals learn:

- To breathe deeply again,
- To sit with their emotions without fear,
- To allow their body to release what it has held too long,
- To reclaim rest,
- And to invite the holy spirit into the tension.

The body remembers pain—but it also responds to peace.

4. Emotional Integration: Permission to Feel, Permission to Heal

Many believers were taught to be strong at the expense of being honest. But emotional suppression blocks spiritual transformation.

Jesus wept. David lamented. Jeremiah mourned. Hannah poured out her soul.

Emotion is not evidence of weakness; emotion is evidence of humanity.

In counseling, individuals learn:

- To cry without shame,
- To lament without guilt,
- To question without fear,
- To acknowledge anger,

- To name disappointment,
- To express confusion in the presence of God.

Breakthrough happens when emotions finally find expression instead of imprisonment.

5. Forgiveness as Restoration: Setting the Heart Free from the Past

Forgiveness is one of the deepest breakthroughs that emerges from brokenness.

This includes:

- Forgiving someone who caused harm,
- Forgiving a system that failed you,
- Forgiving a season that wounded you,
- Forgiving yourself for surviving the best way you knew how.

Forgiveness does not erase history—it removes the weight of history from your future.

Scripture affirms this: "**He heals the brokenhearted and binds up their wounds.**" (Psalm 147:3)

Forgiveness turns brokenness into blessing.

6. Post-Traumatic Growth: Finding Purpose in the Pieces

Therapeutically, "post-traumatic growth" describes the new strength, wisdom, and purpose that emerge *after* suffering.

Spiritually, it is Joseph's declaration: "**You meant it for evil, but God meant it for good.**" (Genesis 50:20)

Growth after brokenness may look like:

- Deeper empathy
- Increased spiritual sensitivity
- Renewed purpose
- Stronger boundaries
- Clearer self-worth
- A calling birthed from pain
- Ministry emerging from scars

Jesus rose *with* His scars—not despite them.

Your scars are not signs of defeat—they are signs of divine survival.

7. Scriptural Anchoring: God Builds with Broken Pieces

Every therapeutic principle is mirrored in Scripture:

- **Trauma-informed care** → "He binds up wounds." (Psalm 147:3)

- **Cognitive reframing** → "Be transformed by the renewing of your mind." (Rom. 12:2)
- **Somatic awareness** → "Be still…" (Psalm 46:10)
- **Emotional integration** → "Pour out your heart before Him." (Psalm 62:8)
- **Forgiveness** → "Forgive as Christ forgave you." (Col. 3:13)
- **Post-traumatic growth** → "After you have suffered a while… He will strengthen and settle you." (1 Peter 5:10)

God is not intimidated by brokenness—He specializes in it.

Pastoral Summary

From the counseling chair, I see brokenness not as a dead end, but as a doorway.

Brokenness is:

- The cracking open of the soul,
- The moment pride gives way to surrender,
- The place where healing begins,
- The soil where empathy grows,
- The humble ground where ministry is born.

Brokenness becomes breakthrough when you allow God into the places you once hid.

Declaration

I am not defined by what broke me but by Who rebuilt me. My cracks are carriers of compassion. Beauty has been born from my brokenness, and purpose has replaced my pain.

Closing Benediction for the Week

"He has made everything beautiful in its time." — Ecclesiastes 3:11 (NKJV)

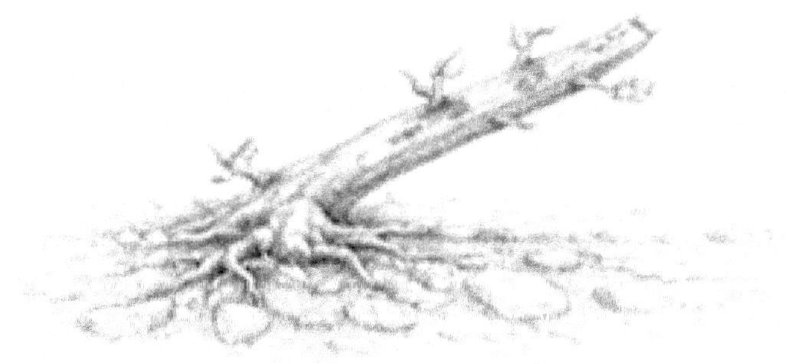

Chapter 7: Stillness in the Silent Season

Be still, and know that I am God."— **Psalm 46:10 (NKJV)**

Exegetical Note:

The command *"Be still"* comes from the Hebrew verb ***rāphâ*** — meaning *"to cease striving, to let go, to loosen the grip."* It does **not** mean inactivity; it means inner surrender. God is not asking for silence of circumstance, but for silence of *spirit* — the quieting of worry, fear, and hurriedness.

The phrase *"know that I am God"* uses the Hebrew ***yāda*‘** — "to know by experience, to acknowledge through encounter." God invites His people not to intellectual awareness, but experiential confidence: **You will know Me best when you stop trying to manage what only I can move.**

Stillness is not passive resignation. It is active trust.

Historical Context:

Psalm 46 was written to a people surrounded by political instability, military threat, and national anxiety. Many scholars connect this psalm to the era of King Hezekiah, when the Assyrian army surrounded Jerusalem (2 Kings 18–19).

While the nation panicked, God declared, "Be still." While enemies advanced, God said, "I will be exalted." The silence God demanded was not because the situation was small — but because **He was sovereign**.

Israel did nothing but trust — and God delivered.

This psalm became a national anthem of assurance: When the world shakes, God stands.

Pastoral Insight:

Silent seasons are not signs of God's absence — they are signals of His strategy. When God quiets your environment, He is often preparing your destiny.

We want God to speak loudly, but He often whispers because whispers require closeness.

Stillness teaches what movement cannot:

- How to hear God beyond the noise
- How to discern His presence beyond emotion
- How to rest in His timing without fear

Winter stillness is not emptiness. It is incubation. God is forming what you cannot see.

And when the season shifts, what He grew in silence will appear in strength.

Be still — not because nothing is happening, but because God is.

Winter is the season of stillness. The world grows quiet, the branches bare, and the soil rests. Many see this as emptiness, but spiritually it is preparation. "Be still, and know that I am God" (Psalm 46:10 NKJV).

Stillness does not mean inactivity—it means intentional trust. It is in the quiet that God often does His deepest work. During these times, He recalibrates our hearts, restores our perspective, and revives our strength. Silence is not the absence of progress; it is the sacred space where growth takes root beneath the surface.

We tend to equate silence with absence, but heaven often speaks in whispers. The absence of noise does not mean the absence of God. Think of Elijah, who sought God in the wind, the earthquake, and the fire—but found Him in a still small voice (1 Kings 19:11–12). When life goes quiet, it is often because God desires to speak differently. He lowers the volume of the world so that His whisper can reach the soul.

In winter, we learn to stop striving and start listening. We realize that productivity is not proof of purpose. Waiting becomes worship. And worship in the dark build's faith for the dawn. It is in these silent seasons that we learn to lean into God's presence rather than our plans. The frost that settles around us does not mean the harvest is over—it means the soil is being renewed for what's next.

Sometimes God will allow the noise of life to fade so we can rediscover the melody of His voice. The still season teaches us that we are not sustained by movement but by mercy. We are reminded that peace is not found in progress but in proximity—being near to the One who never leaves. "The Lord will fight for you; you need only to be still" (Exodus 14:14). Stillness is not passive—it is power restrained by faith.

When we enter a silent season, our first instinct is often to fill the space—with words, with activity, with distraction. But spiritual stillness calls us to resist the urge to fix and simply *be*. The soil cannot yield new growth until it rests. Likewise, our souls cannot produce fresh fruit until they find rest in God. Winter invites us to trust what we cannot see and to believe that beneath the frozen ground, new life is forming.

Stillness also refines our hearing. When we stop speaking, we start perceiving. In the silence, we hear God's heart again. He reveals the motives behind our movements, the healing needed for our hearts, and the wisdom required for our next steps. What feels like delay is often divine alignment—God ordering what was once out of place.

When you find yourself in a silent season, resist the urge to panic. What looks like pause is often protection. God hides us to heal us, shelters us to strengthen us, and quiets us so that we might hear Him clearly again. A cocoon may seem like confinement to the caterpillar, but it is actually the womb of transformation. In silence, wings are forming.

There is also beauty in God's timing of silence. Just as snow blankets the earth to insulate and preserve, His stillness shields our spirit while He prepares our next assignment. You may not hear His voice as you once did, but His hand is still guiding. Trust that the same God who spoke in the last season is still present in this one. The silence is not punishment—it is preservation.

When the world feels cold and motionless, remember that the God of every season has not forgotten you. What He began in spring, He sustains through winter. The same Spirit who whispered in the warmth still watches in the cold. Stillness teaches us that survival is not in striving but in surrender.

Soon, the thaw will come, and what was resting will rise again. But for now, embrace the quiet. Let peace wrap around your heart like a winter blanket. Let faith warm what fear tried to freeze. Be still, and know that even in the silence, God is still speaking, still shaping, still sustaining.

Do not despise this season. The quiet of winter is not the end of growth—it's the rest that makes new growth possible. God's greatest miracles often begin in moments of stillness: a womb, a tomb, an upper room. The hush before the resurrection is holy.

The silent season is sacred space. Let it teach you to breathe again, to trust again, and to see that even in the absence of sound, God's presence is enough.

Vignette: The Choir Without a Song

Vonda had sung in her church choir for thirty years. But after losing her husband, she lost her song. She attended rehearsals but couldn't bring herself to sing. Every hymn felt heavy, every melody a reminder of what she'd lost. One day, her director noticed and gently said, "You don't have to sing today. Just listen."

For weeks, she sat in silence, surrounded by the harmonics of others. She began to realize that though her voice was still, the music continued around her. God hadn't stopped the song—He was simply inviting her to rest in the rhythm.

Months later, as the choir sang *"It Is Well with My Soul,"* tears streamed down her face. Without forcing it, her voice joined theirs again—soft but strong.

Later she said, "I thought silence was my end, but it became my healing."

God's quiet is never empty; it's full of His presence, waiting for the moment our hearts are ready to sing again.

Reflection: The Gift of Sacred Silence

Stillness is a language God speaks fluently. He uses silence to reset our pace and reframe our purpose. In the noise of striving, we often miss His whispers of direction. Silence sharpens our hearing.

Ask yourself: *What is God trying to show me in this quiet?* Perhaps He's healing wounds too deep for words. Perhaps He's preparing answers that require time. The silence isn't proof that He's gone—it's proof that He's working on something sacred.

Stillness is not inactivity; it's incubation. When you learn to rest in His rhythm, you begin to recognize that peace isn't found in progress but in presence.

Life Application: Learning to Rest in God's Quiet

1. **Schedule silence.** Create intentional pauses in your day. Even five minutes of stillness can refresh your spirit.

2. **Quiet your mind with Scripture.** Read one psalm slowly, out loud. Let its words still your thoughts.

3. **Stop explaining and start expecting.** Instead of rehearsing your frustrations in prayer, rest in faith that God already knows.

4. **Find peace in hiddenness.** Trust that being unseen does not mean being forgotten.

5. **Guard your spiritual rest.** Don't rush out of winter. Let it do its work. Spring will come when the soil of your heart is ready. Stillness is an act of faith that says, *"Even when I don't move, God does."*

Closing Prayer

Heavenly Father, Thank You for the sacred stillness that restores my soul. When I cannot hear You, help me trust that You are near. Quiet my anxious thoughts and teach me to rest in Your peace. Let my waiting be worship and my silence be surrender. Renew my strength in the hidden place and prepare me for the new beginnings ahead. In Jesus' name, Amen.

Appendix G — Devotional Companion: Stillness in the Silent Season

Key Scripture: *"Be still, and know that I am God."*— **Psalm 46:10 (NKJV)**

Purpose of this Devotional: This companion invites you to rest in God's quiet work. Silence is not a punishment; it's preparation. Stillness helps us hear His whisper above the world's noise.

Day 1 — When Heaven Seems Quiet

Scripture: Psalm 13:1

Reflection: Even David wondered how long God would be silent. Silence tests trust but builds intimacy.

Practice: Write one unanswered prayer and surrender it again to God today.

Prayer: *Lord, when I cannot hear You, help me trust that You are still speaking in my silence.*

Day 2 — Listening Beneath the Noise

Scripture: 1 Kings 19:11–12

Reflection: God's voice was not in the earthquake or fire, but in the whisper. He often chooses stillness to speak to the soul.

Practice: Spend ten minutes in complete quiet—no phone, no music. Simply breathe and listen.

Prayer: *Holy Spirit, tune my heart to hear Your still, small voice.*

Day 3 — The Ministry of Waiting

Scripture: Isaiah 40:31

Reflection: Waiting is worship when we wait with expectation. In delay, God develops strength.

Practice: List one lesson you've learned during a waiting season.

Prayer: *Lord, renew my strength as I wait for Your perfect timing.*

Day 4 — Rest for the Restless Heart

Scripture: Matthew 11:28–29

Reflection: Rest is not inactivity—it's trust. When you rest in Christ, you release the burden of outcomes.

Practice: Schedule a moment of rest today: a walk, a prayer, or five deep breaths in His presence.

Prayer: *Jesus, calm my heart and teach me to find rest in Your yoke.*

Day 5 — Faith in the Fog

Scripture: Hebrews 11:1

Reflection: Faith thrives in uncertainty. When the path is hidden, trust becomes the map.

Practice: Draw or write a symbol that represents faith for you. Keep it where you can see it.

Prayer: *Father, help me walk by faith, not by sight, and trust You even in the fog.*

Day 6 — Hidden but Held

Scripture: Exodus 33:22

Reflection: Sometimes God hides us in the cleft for protection, not punishment. Hidden seasons are holy shields.

Practice: Reflect on one season where God's "no" was really His protection.

Prayer: *Thank You, Lord, for covering me until the right moment to reveal me.*

Day 7 — The Sound of Surrender

Scripture: Philippians 4:6–7

Reflection: Peace is the sound of a surrendered soul. When we stop striving, His stillness fills the space.

Practice: End this week by writing a prayer of surrender.

Prayer: *God, quiet my anxious thoughts and fill me with Your peace that surpasses understanding.*

Pastoral Counseling Lens - From the Counseling Chair

Silence is one of the most misunderstood seasons of spiritual life. In counseling, I often meet individuals who say, "I can't hear God anymore," interpreting His quietness as abandonment or disapproval. But biblically and therapeutically, silence is not the absence of God—it is the environment where God does His deepest internal shaping.

Silent seasons are sacred seasons.

1. Anxiety Reduction: Replacing Noise with Nurture

When life becomes quiet, anxiety often gets louder. Without external distractions, unresolved fears rise to the surface:

- "What if God has forgotten me?"
- "What if nothing changes?"
- "What if I missed God's will?"
- "What if I'm stuck like this forever?"

CBT teaches that anxiety thrives in ambiguity. But Scripture answers ambiguity with assurance:

"Be still, and know that I am God." (Psalm 46:10)

In counseling, I help individuals:

- Identify anxious thought patterns
- Challenge catastrophic thinking
- Practice breath prayer
- Develop mindful stillness
- Replace "what if?" With "God is."

Stillness is not the absence of movement—it is the presence of trust.

2. Cognitive Reframing: Silence Is Not Absence

Many misinterpret God's quiet seasons as distance. This belief shapes emotional responses:

- Sadness
- Insecurity
- Discouragement
- Self-doubt
- Spiritual confusion

But Scripture reframes silence:

- Elijah heard God in the still small voice (1 Kings 19).
- Jesus often withdrew into silent places (Luke 5:16).
- Habakkuk stood "upon the watch" in silence before God responded.

Reframed Truth:

When God is silent, He is not absent—He is working in the unseen.

Instead of "God isn't speaking," the truth becomes: *"God is preparing me to hear differently."*

Instead of "Nothing is happening," the truth becomes: *"Something is being refined beneath the surface."*

Silence becomes sanctuary when seen through God's lens.

3. Attachment Healing: Learning to Trust Without Constant Reassurance

Silent seasons often trigger attachment wounds. A heart familiar with abandonment may interpret God's quietness as rejection.

In counseling, individuals learn to:

- Differentiate divine silence from human absence
- Separate God's character from past relational wounds
- Trust his presence without constant emotional confirmation

God's character remains constant even when His voice seems still:

"I will never leave you nor forsake you." (Hebrews 13:5)

Silent seasons stretch believers toward **secure attachment** with Christ—rooted not in emotion, but in truth.

4. Emotional Regulation: Sitting with Yourself, Not Running from Yourself

Silence forces self-awareness. It reveals:

- Stored sadness
- Hidden fears
- Unprocessed grief
- Old memories
- Emotional fatigue
- Internal conflict

Instead of distracting from these emotions, silent seasons invite believers to **sit with themselves before God**.

In counseling, emotional regulation tools support this process:

- Breath work
- Grounding exercises
- Journaling honest prayers
- Meditative scripture reading
- Practicing solitude
- Naming emotions without shame

Stillness becomes soul-restoration rather than soul-strain.

5. Discernment Development: Hearing the God Who Whispers

Silence sharpens discernment.

When life is busy, people hear God through circumstances. When life is loud, they hear God through sermons. But when life becomes silent—they hear God through **whispered revelation**.

In silence, the Spirit reveals:

- Motivations
- Boundaries
- Unhealthy patterns
- Next steps
- Emotional needs
- Divine direction
- Hidden idols

What feels like delay is often divine diagnosis.

Discernment deepens in stillness because distractions diminish.

6. Forgiveness & Release: Silence Exposes What Needs Healing

Silent seasons are often when God reveals:

- Unresolved bitterness

- Secret disappointments
- Subconscious resentment toward God
- Buried anger
- Unspoken grief

Letting these unspoken truths surface opens the door to healing. Stillness becomes the setting where God tenderly asks:

"Will you release this?"

"Will you trust Me here?"

"Will you let Me heal what noise has been numbing?"

Forgiveness—of God, self, or others—often emerges in the quiet.

7. Scriptural Anchoring: God Speaks in Sacred Stillness

Every counseling principle in this chapter is rooted in the Word:

- **Anxiety Reduction** → "Cast all your anxieties…" (1 Peter 5:7)

- **Reframing Silence** → "In quietness… shall be your strength." (Isaiah 30:15)

- **Attachment Security** → "Underneath are the everlasting arms." (Deut. 33:27)

- **Emotional Regulation** → "Let not your heart be troubled." (John 14:1)

- **Discernment** → "My sheep hear my voice." (John 10:27)

- **Forgiveness & Release** → "Create in me a clean heart…" (Psalm 51:10)

God whispers in stillness because whispers require proximity.

Pastoral Summary

From the counseling chair, I see silent seasons not as abandonment, but as divine alignment.

Silence is:

- God shifting your attention
- God recalibrating your emotions
- God deepening your roots
- God preparing new revelation
- God detoxing your soul
- God strengthening your discernment
- God teaching you the language of stillness

In the quiet, God is closest. In the silence, God is shaping. In the stillness, God is speaking.

Declaration

I will not fear the quiet. God is working in my waiting and whispering in my stillness. My peace is proof of His presence.

Closing Benediction for the Week

"In returning and rest you shall be saved; in quietness and confidence shall be your strength."— Isaiah 30:15 (NKJV)

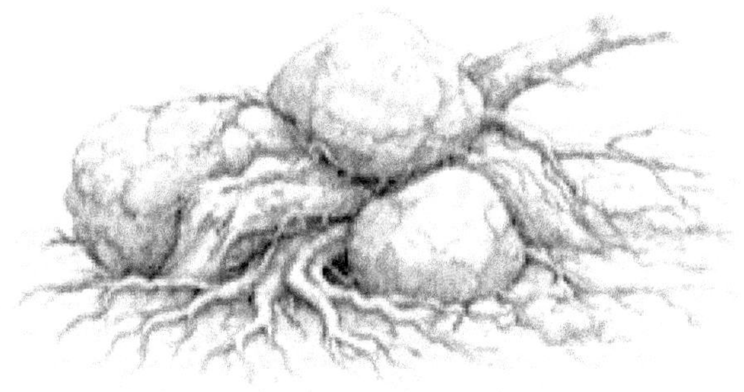

Chapter 8: When God Heals the Heart

"He heals the brokenhearted and binds up their wounds."— **Psalm 147:3 (NKJV)**

Exegetical Note:

The Hebrew verb for *"heals"* is ***rapha'*** — the same root used for God's covenant name *Jehovah Rapha*, "the Lord who heals." It means *to restore, to mend, to make whole.* Healing here is not temporary relief; it is **total repair**.

The phrase *"brokenhearted"* uses the compound Hebrew term ***lishbar lev*** — literally "a heart shattered into pieces." The psalmist is describing emotional devastation so deep that only divine intervention can reach it.

The words *"binds up"* translate the Hebrew ***ḥabash*** — "to bandage, wrap, cover, or dress a wound." It is the language of a careful physician. God is pictured not as a distant deity but as a gentle healer who kneels at the bedside of the hurting, touching what others avoid.

Historical Context:

Psalm 147 was written after Israel returned from Babylonian exile — a collective trauma marked by loss, displacement, and disillusionment. The people rebuilt walls and cities, but their hearts were still in ruins.

This psalm proclaims that **God heals the internal before He restores the external**. It celebrates a God who is attentive to the wounded, present with the grieving, and patient with the recovering.

Israel had been uprooted, crushed, and scattered. Now, in their season of rebuilding, the psalmist reminds them: **Your healing is not self-made; it is God-given.**

The God who gathers the outcasts (v. 2) is the same God who gathers the fragments of a broken heart.

Pastoral Insight:

Healing is rarely instant and never accidental. It unfolds layer by layer, just as God restores us breath by breath, truth by truth, surrender by surrender.

We often expect healing to look like the reversal of pain, but God's healing is deeper: It transforms the pain, reframes the memory, and restores meaning.

A healed heart does not forget what happened — it no longer bleeds from it.

Healing begins where resistance ends. When we stop pretending, we're fine and start presenting our wounds to God, He binds what we bring and restores what we release.

Scars are not signs of failure — they are signs of survival. They tell the world, "God met me here."

Healing is not the return to who you were — it is the unveiling of who you've become.

Healing rarely happens in haste. Like the first signs of spring peeking through winter snow, the heart heals gradually—layer by layer, prayer by prayer. "He heals the brokenhearted and binds up their wounds" (Psalm 147:3 NKJV). Healing is both a process and a promise. It is God's gentle way of reminding us that time in His hands is never wasted. It is His tender invitation to trade pain for peace and despair for hope.

There's a moment when we realize that God's healing doesn't always mean things return to the way they were. Sometimes, healing is learning to live fully in a new way. The scar remains, but the pain is gone—and the mark becomes a testimony of grace. What once symbolized suffering becomes evidence of survival. Just as Christ's resurrected body bore scars that testified of victory, your healing tells the world that what was meant to destroy you became the place of your divine encounter and your scars tell the world that God's grace outlasts every wound.

Emotional healing mirrors physical healing: both require rest, patience, and gentle care. The soul cannot rush recovery. We often want immediate relief, but God desires enduring restoration. When you bring your pain into His presence, He begins to replace sorrow with strength, confusion with clarity, and emptiness with expectancy. Healing begins where striving ends.

Sometimes, the heart's deepest wounds are invisible. They are hidden beneath smiles, routines, and responsibilities. We keep moving, hoping the motion will muffle the ache. But the only way to heal is to feel—and to surrender those feelings to the hands of the One who created the heart in the first place. The Holy Spirit moves tenderly through our pain, not to remind us of loss, but to reveal that nothing is beyond His touch.

God's process is deliberate. He may begin by healing the mind, transforming the way we think about what happened. "Be transformed by the renewing of your mind" (Romans 12:2). Then He softens the emotions, teaching us to forgive what once seemed unforgivable. Finally, He renews the spirit, giving us courage to live again without fear. Healing is holistic; it reaches every layer of who we are.

God's process is tender. Sometimes, He first quiets the storm within before addressing the circumstances around you. The Holy Spirit moves through the cracks of our pain like light through stained glass, illuminating the broken places with beauty. The pieces that once seemed shattered begin to reflect His glory in ways they never could when life was whole and untested.

Healing the heart involves forgiveness—not just toward others, but toward yourself. Many remain bound by guilt long after God has declared them free. Remember His words: "As far as the east is from the west, so far has He removed our transgressions from us" (Psalm 103:12 NKJV). True healing begins when we stop revisiting what God has already redeemed. When God forgives, He forgets. Yet we often carry memories as though His mercy were conditional. True healing comes when we stop rehearsing the pain and start releasing it.

Forgiveness does not erase memory; it redeems it. It changes how the memory feels. What once stung now strengthens. What once haunted now humbles. Forgiveness clears the clutter of resentment so that peace can take root again.

God heals by restoring perspective. What once seemed like ruin becomes revelation. What once broke you now builds you. He takes every tear and transforms it into testimony. Healing is not about erasing the past—it's about seeing it through redeemed eyes. You begin to thank God, not for the pain, but for what it produced: deeper empathy, stronger faith, and unshakable trust.

There are moments in healing when memories resurface unexpectedly—when a song, a scent, or a place awakens old wounds. Don't interpret these moments as setbacks; see them as invitations to deeper wholeness. Each time you bring that memory back to God, He layers it with more grace until the sting is gone and only wisdom remains.

God heals by restoring perspective. What once seemed like ruin becomes revelation. What once broke you now builds you. He takes every tear and transforms it into testimony. Healing is not about erasing the past—it's about seeing it through redeemed eyes. You begin to thank God, not for the pain, but for what it produced: deeper empathy, stronger faith, and unshakable peace.

Sometimes, God heals by subtraction. He removes people, habits, or environments that reopen the wound. Other times, He heals by addition—sending new relationships, opportunities, or ministries to remind you that life is not over. Either way, His goal is not to return you to who you were but to reveal who you've become. Healing is resurrection in slow motion.

Healing doesn't mean you stop missing what was; it means you start embracing what is. It's not pretending the hurt didn't happen; it's proclaiming that it no longer controls you. God heals so you can help others heal. The comfort you receive becomes the comfort you extend: "Who comforts us in all our tribulation, that we may be able to comfort those who are in any trouble" (2 Corinthians 1:4).

When God heals the heart, He doesn't just mend what's broken—He redefines what's beautiful.

As the heart mends, gratitude becomes your daily companion. You start to notice beauty again—the laughter that once felt distant, the sunrise that reminds you that light always returns after darkness. You learn that healing doesn't mean forgetting, but it does mean moving forward without fear.

And when healing is complete, you'll realize it was never just for you. God restores so you can reach others. The comfort you received becomes the comfort you give. "Blessed be the God… who comforts us in all our tribulation, that we may be able to comfort those who are in any trouble" (2 Corinthians 1:3–4). Your healed heart becomes an instrument of hope in the hands of a faithful God.

Vignette: The Bookbinder's Gift

Malcolm owned an old Bible that had belonged to his grandmother. Its pages were frayed, the spine cracked, and several sections were loose from years of use. He considered replacing it, but something in his spirit whispered, *"Repair it instead."*

He took it to a professional bookbinder—an elderly man who had spent decades restoring antique volumes. The craftsman studied the Bible with care and said, "I can't make it look new, but I can make it whole."

Weeks later, when Malcolm picked it up, tears filled his eyes. The pages were still aged, but the binding was strong. The gold lettering had been restored. The marks of time remained—but the book had been given new life.

That night, as Malcolm read from its pages, he felt the Lord speak to his heart: *"That's what I've done with you. I didn't erase your story; I restored it."*

He realized healing wasn't about pretending the tears had never fallen—it was about knowing that God had carefully rebound the pages, making the testimony even more valuable than before.

Reflection: The Pace of Healing

Healing is holy work. It cannot be hurried because it's not just about feeling better—it's about becoming whole. The same God who created your heart knows how to restore it. You may feel impatient, but God is not slow; He is thorough.

Ask yourself: *Where am I still rushing what requires rest?* Healing happens in His timing, not ours. Like the blooming of a flower, every layer opens at the right time. The petals of joy will unfold again, but only after the roots of faith have been watered.

Be patient with yourself. God's healing is unfolding in ways you can't yet see.

Life Application: Walking in Healing

1. **Be honest with your heart.** Healing begins with truth. Tell God how you feel without filters—He can handle it.

2. **Stop rehearsing the hurt.** Each time you relive the pain, you reopen the wound. Replace repetition with renewal—speak the Word instead.

3. **Forgive intentionally.** Write down the names, situations, or regrets you've carried. Pray over them, release them, and let peace replace bitterness.

4. **Rest in grace.** Healing doesn't require performance. Some days you'll move forward; other days you'll just breathe. Both are progress.

5. **Remember your Healer.** Don't glorify the wound—glorify the One who healed it. Keep your focus on the restorer, not the ruin.

Healing is not the end of your story—it's the turning of a page toward purpose.

Closing Prayer

Heavenly Healer, Thank You for mending my broken heart with Your love. Teach me to be patient with Your process. Help me to forgive others and myself, to release bitterness, and to trust that You are restoring me from the inside out. May my scars shine as symbols of Your mercy. Heal me completely—spirit, soul, and body—so I can help others find their healing in You. In Jesus' name, Amen.

Appendix H — Devotional Companion: When God Heals the Heart

Key Scripture: *"He heals the brokenhearted and binds up their wounds."*— **Psalm 147:3 (NKJV)**

The Purpose of the Devotional:

Healing is a journey, not a single moment. This devotional companion invites you to walk with God through the gradual process of mending—where every tear becomes testimony and every scar reveals His grace.

Day 1 — The Gentle Healer

Scripture: Matthew 11:28–29

Reflection: God heals with gentleness. He doesn't rush our recovery; He restores at a rhythm that matches His grace.

Practice: Take five quiet minutes to breathe deeply and whisper, "I am safe in Your healing hands."

Prayer: *Lord, soothe the tender places of my heart and teach me to rest in Your timing.*

Day 2 — Facing the Wound

Scripture: Psalm 139:23–24

Reflection: God can only heal what we're willing to expose. Honest confession opens the door to deep restoration.

Practice: Journal one hidden pain or disappointment you've been afraid to face.

Prayer: *Father, search my heart and shine light on what still needs Your touch.*

Day 3 — The Courage to Forgive

Scripture: Mark 11:25

Reflection: Forgiveness is not excusing the offense—it's releasing the offender to God. True healing begins where resentment ends.

Practice: Pray specifically for someone who hurt you, asking God to bless them

Prayer: *Lord, free me from bitterness so that Your love can freely flow through me.*

Day 4 — Healing the Inner Voice

Scripture: Romans 12:2

Reflection: Sometimes our wounds speak louder than God's Word. Renewing the mind silences lies with truth.

Practice: Write down one negative thought you often believe. Replace it with a Scripture promise.

Prayer: *God, reframe my thoughts with Your truth and restore my confidence in Your Word.*

Day 5 — Forgiving Yourself

Scripture: 1 John 1:9

Reflection: Guilt keeps the wound open. Grace closes it. When God forgives, we must learn to forgive ourselves.

Practice: Look in the mirror and say aloud, "I am forgiven and free."

Prayer: *Thank You, Lord, for mercy that covers every mistake and grace that calls me whole.*

Day 6 — The Slow Miracle

Scripture: Philippians 1:6

Reflection: Healing is often slow so that we can learn to depend on the Healer. Every layer restored is a lesson in grace.

Practice: Write one small sign of progress you've noticed in your journey. Celebrate it.

Prayer: *God, thank You for working even when I can't see change. I trust Your process.*

Day 7 — Wholeness Restored

Scripture: Jeremiah 30:17

Reflection: God restores more than health—He restores hope. Wholeness means living again with joy.

Practice: End your week by writing a prayer of thanksgiving for your renewed heart.

Prayer: *Father, thank You for binding my wounds and bringing beauty from my brokenness.*

Heart-healing is one of the most sacred forms of restoration. In counseling, I've learned that emotional wounds do not heal by time alone; they heal through truth, intentionality, spiritual honesty, and the gentle work of the Holy Spirit. Healing is not linear. It is layered, patterned, and profoundly intimate.

This chapter explores how God partners with our emotional and psychological processes to restore the heart.

Pastoral Counseling Lens - From the Counseling Chair

1. Trauma Integration: Healing the Layer Beneath the Hurt

Pain leaves imprints—on memory, on emotion, and sometimes even on the body. Many individuals believe they are "over it," but their reactions tell another story:

- Sudden emotional flooding
- Difficulty trusting
- Fear of vulnerability
- Overthinking
- Shutting down
- Avoiding affection
- Expecting abandonment

Trauma integration involves helping individuals understand that:

- Triggers are unprocessed echoes

- Emotional patterns are survival strategies
- God does not despise their fragility
- Healing is possible even for deep wounds

Scripture affirms God's role in trauma healing:

"**He heals the brokenhearted and binds up their wounds.**" (Psalm 147:3)

Healing does not erase the past—it integrates the past into a redeemed identity.

2. Cognitive Reframing: Rewriting the Beliefs Pain Created

Emotional wounds often produce distorted beliefs such as:

- "I'm not worth loving."
- "Pain is my destiny."
- "Joy isn't for people like me."
- "Every good thing ends."
- "Healing happens for others, not me."

CBT reframing helps individuals examine these thoughts through the lens of truth.

Reframed Truths:

- "I am loved with an everlasting love." (Jer. 31:3)

- "My story is not defined by sorrow."
- "God restores the years the locusts have eaten." (Joel 2:25)
- "I can hope again."
- "Healing is my inheritance."

God heals the heart by renewing the mind.

3. Somatic Release: Letting the Body Exhale What the Heart Has Been Holding

The heart and body are connected. Emotional pain often manifests physically:

- Chest tightness
- Fatigue
- Insomnia
- Headaches
- Tension in the shoulders
- Shallow breathing

Somatic counseling techniques teach individuals to release emotional memory stored in the body.

Practices include:

- Breath prayer
- Grounding techniques
- Slow, mindful breathing
- Gentle stretching

- Naming where the pain lives in the body
- Inviting God into physical tension

David prayed, "**Let my soul live, and it shall praise You.**" Healing touches soul and body, not one without the other.

4. Forgiveness & Self-Compassion: Healing the Inner Critic

Many people struggle to heal because they battle an internal accuser.

The inner critic says:

- "This is your fault."
- "You should be further by now."
- "You're too broken."
- "You ruined your chances for joy."

In counseling, we practice:

- Self-compassion
- Grace-filled self-talk
- Releasing unrealistic expectations
- Forgiving oneself for what was done in survival mode
- Accepting god's kindness

Scripture anchors this practice:
"**As far as the east is from the west…**" (Psalm 103:12)

Self-forgiveness is not indulgent—it is spiritual alignment with God's mercy.

5. Rebuilding Trust: Learning to Hold Hope Again

Heart wounds often assault hope:

- "What if it happens again?"
- "Why trust anyone?"
- "Why try again?"
- "Why open myself to love?"

Healing requires rebuilding trust in:

- God's sovereignty
- God's timing
- God's protection
- God's ability to restore
- God's knowledge of your heart's needs

Hope is not naïve—it is biblical.
"**Hope does not disappoint.**" (Romans 5:5)

Hope is the oxygen of healing.

6. Relational Repair: Allowing Safe People into the Healing Process

No heart heals in isolation.
In counseling, I remind individuals:

- Safe community accelerates healing.
- Vulnerability strengthens resilience.
- Healthy relationships re-teach the heart what love feels like.

God often heals through:

- Godly friendships
- Supportive family
- Pastoral care
- Therapeutic alliance
- Spiritual mentors
- Healthy romantic relationships in god's timing

Healing requires safe presence.
Even Jesus allowed His inner circle into Gethsemane.

7. Scriptural Anchoring: Healing Is God's Specialty

Every therapeutic principle in this chapter mirrors God's Word:

- **Trauma Integration** → "He binds up wounds." (Psalm 147:3)

- **Reframing** → "Be transformed by renewing your mind." (Rom. 12:2)
- **Somatic Healing** → "He restores my soul." (Psalm 23:3)
- **Self-Compassion** → "There is no condemnation…" (Rom. 8:1)
- **Rebuilding Trust** → "I know the plans I have for you…" (Jer. 29:11)
- **Relational Repair** → "Carry one another's burdens." (Gal. 6:2) Healing is not merely recovery—it is resurrection.

Pastoral Summary

From the counseling chair, I have seen many hearts heal, often beginning with the smallest acts of surrender.

Heart healing is:

- A divine exchange of sorrow for strength,
- A lifting of emotional weight,
- A renewing of hope,
- A restoration of identity,
- A gentle reprioritizing of what matters,
- And a beautiful unveiling of resilience.

When God heals the heart, He does not just repair it—He restores it with purpose, compassion, and renewed capacity for love.

Declaration

My heart is healing in God's hands. I am not my past, nor my pain. Grace has rewoven what was torn, and peace now guards what once bled.

Closing Benediction for the Week

"As far as the east is from the west, so far has He removed our transgressions from us."— Psalm 103:12 (NKJV)

Part 3: The New Spring

This is the season of becoming again.

Every ending in God is only the beginning of something greater. Winter has done its work—quietly refining, pruning, and restoring. Now, as the final frost melts away, a new spring dawns—not just in nature, but in your soul.

The same God who carried you through storms now calls you to step into sunlight. The soil of your life, once barren, is fertile again with hope. You've survived the silence, endured the stillness, and learned the sacred rhythm of surrender. Now, new life begins to bloom in the very places you thought were beyond repair.

Spring represents resurrection. *It whispers the eternal truth that nothing surrendered to God ever truly dies—it is simply replanted in purpose. What fell away in autumn and lay dormant in winter is now being reborn with brilliance and beauty. The branches that were bare now stretch heavenward, clothed in green once more.*

This new spring is not about returning to what was; it's about becoming what's next. The old patterns no longer fit. The old fears no longer bind. You've learned that growth is not about striving but abiding—resting in the assurance that God is faithful to finish what He began.

You are not who you were when the journey began. The tests that once terrified you have become testimonies. The tears that watered the ground have produced grace-filled fruit. The waiting that wearied you has made you wise. You have emerged more rooted, more radiant, more resilient.

In this new spring, walk gently but boldly. Let peace be your pace. Let gratitude be your garment. Let grace be your ground. This is not just a season of restoration—it is a season of revelation. God is revealing who you've become through the process, and it is beautiful to behold.

The Psalmist said, "Those who sow in tears shall reap in joy" *(Psalm 126:5 NKJV). You are standing now in your reaping season. Joy is sprouting from sorrow. Purpose is growing from pain. The garden of your soul is alive again, fragrant with promise and full of possibility.*

As you step into this new spring, remember—this is not a second chance; it is a continuing grace. *You do not have to rebuild the way things were; you are invited to bloom into who you were always meant to be.*

The winds of the past no longer shake you. The weight of yesterday no longer defines you. You've been pruned, planted, and prepared—and now, it's time to flourish.

Lift your eyes, beloved of God. The season of wholeness is here. The long winter has passed, and the voice of the Lord is calling you forward: ***"Arise, my love, my fair one, and come away. For lo, the winter is past, the rain is over and gone"*** *(Song of Solomon 2:10–11 NKJV).*

Step into your New Spring. *The world needs the fragrance of what God has grown in you.*

Live whole. Live holy. And live fully alive in the garden of His grace.

Chapter 9: Love Beyond the Ashes

"To console those who mourn in Zion, to give them beauty for ashes, The oil of joy for mourning, The garment of praise for the spirit of heaviness; That they may be called trees of righteousness, The planting of the Lord, that He may be glorified."— **Isaiah 61:3 (NKJVa)**

Exegetical Note:

The word *"beauty"* comes from the Hebrew ***pe'er*** — meaning *a headdress, a crown, or an ornament of dignity.* It was a symbol of honor worn during celebrations. The Lord promises not simply to remove ashes but to **replace them with royalty**.

"Ashes" (*'ēpher*) represent grief, repentance, and the residue of things burned beyond recognition. They symbolize what life has taken, what loss has left behind, and what sorrow has scattered.

The exchange is divine:

- **Ashes** → Crown
- **Mourning** → Oil of joy
- **Heaviness** → Garment of praise

The word *"heaviness"* (*kēhâ*) implies dimness of spirit — a soul whose flame has nearly gone out. God doesn't demand brightness—He restores it.

The term *"trees of righteousness"* uses the Hebrew ***oaks*** (*'ēlê*) — trees known for deep roots and extraordinary longevity. Restoration is not temporary; it is designed to last.

Historical Context:

Isaiah 61 is a prophetic announcement to Israel after the devastation of exile. Cities lay in ruins, families were fractured, and identity was shaken. Into this brokenness, God speaks a message of dramatic restoration.

Centuries later, Jesus reads this very passage in the synagogue (Luke 4:16–21), declaring that **He is the fulfillment of this promise**. He is the One who turns loss into legacy, mourning into meaning, and ashes into anointing.

The message is both historical and eternal: God does not end stories in devastation. He rebuilds. He restores. He resurrects.

Pastoral Insight:

Love after loss is not a replacement of what was; it is the redemption of what remains. Ashes represent moments that should have destroyed you — yet here you are. Breathing. Hoping. Healing.

God does not rush you through your ashes. He sits with you in them. And when the time is right, He rebuilds you from them.

Many fear loving again because they assume new love dishonors old grief. But Scripture teaches the opposite: **When God restores, He multiplies.** He transforms the burned places into blessed places.

Love beyond the ashes is careful but courageous. It remembers the past but is not imprisoned by it. It honors what was but embraces what is becoming.

God doesn't hand you back what burned. He hands you what's been resurrected.

There is life after loss and love beyond the ashes. God never ends a story with ashes; He writes redemption into every line. "To grant to those who mourn in Zion—to give them beauty for ashes, the oil of joy for mourning, the garment of praise for the spirit of heaviness" (Isaiah 61:3 NKJV).

When God restores, He does more than replace—He renews. Renewal means new joy, new hope, new purpose. It's the realization that your worth was never lost in what left you. The ashes of what once was become the foundation for what can be. Like a phoenix rising, your heart learns to soar again—not because the past is forgotten, but because God has breathed new life into the ruins. God takes the residue of disappointment and turns it into revelation.

This chapter explores learning to love again—yourself, your calling, and, when God ordains it, another person. Renewal teaches gratitude for grace. The one who has been forgiven much loves much (Luke 7:47). After pain, love becomes purer, guided not by need but by wisdom.

Love reborn after heartbreak is tender yet discerning. It knows the cost of trust and values the sacredness of peace. It's a love that no longer seeks validation, but instead overflows from a healed heart.

Love beyond the ashes isn't reckless—it's redeemed. It's love that knows pain but chooses peace; love that trusts again because God has healed the heart. Your past is not a prison—it's preparation for compassion, understanding, and balance. You learn to see yourself and others through the lens of grace instead of guilt.

When you've walked through fire and survived, you love differently. You no longer mistake attention for affection or chaos for connection. Love that rises from ashes is anchored in discernment. It doesn't need validation to feel valued. It flows from a healed heart that knows: *I am loved by God first.*

God often uses broken seasons to reveal what real love looks like. Love that lasts is not built on perfection but on prayer. It's not sustained by emotion but by endurance. The heart that has been refined through trial becomes fertile soil for healthy relationships. What once was naive becomes wise; what once was fearful becomes faithful.

When God restores love, He doesn't simply resurrect what was; He creates something altogether new. "Behold, I make all things new" (Revelation 21:5). Learning to love again begins with loving yourself through God's eyes. Too often, we see ourselves through the lens of failure or rejection, forgetting that grace has rewritten our identity. You are not the mistakes you made or the heartbreak you endured. You are the masterpiece still being painted by the Master's hand. When you accept His unconditional love, you no longer chase after people to fill what only His presence can satisfy.

Then comes the courage to love life again. After loss, even joy can feel foreign at first. It takes faith to laugh again, to dream again, to open your heart again. But God's Word reminds us that "weeping may endure for a night, but joy comes in the morning" (Psalm 30:5). Morning doesn't erase the night—it redeems it. You learn that joy can coexist with memory, and peace can flourish where pain once lived.

For those whom God calls to love again in relationship, it's important to understand that new love is not a replacement—it's a revelation. It reveals how deeply God can heal, how beautifully He can restore, and how faithfully He redeems time. A relationship birthed after ashes should never carry the residue of what was, but rather the fragrance of what's been renewed. It is love reborn through grace, guarded by discernment, and guided by peace.

Before God introduces someone new, He ensures you've been made new. Healing precedes union. When both hearts have been purified by fire, what emerges is gold—love refined, not rushed. A healed person loves differently. They listen more deeply, forgive more easily, and hold more gently. Love becomes less about possession and more about partnership—less about having someone and more about becoming someone who reflects Christ.

Before love returns, God first restores your identity. He teaches you to love yourself the way He loves you—completely, compassionately, and without condition. Self-love in Christ is not arrogance; it's agreement.

It's agreeing with God about who you are. When you begin to see yourself as He does—chosen, redeemed, and worthy—you stop settling for less than covenant love.

If God has called you to love again—whether that's a relationship, a ministry, or a purpose that once seemed burned away—know this: He never rebuilds with ashes; He builds with resurrection. The God who raised Jesus from the grave is the same God who can resurrect joy, peace, and love in you.

When you've walked through ashes, love beyond them requires trust—not only in another person, but in God's plan. You must believe that His timing is perfect and that His restoration is not random. The same God who allowed seasons of pruning will also allow seasons of blooming. You are not behind schedule; you are right where grace intended. Love beyond the ashes is not about repeating old patterns; it's about writing new ones with wisdom. It's the love that prays first, listens longer, and speaks life. It is patient because it remembers pain. It is pure because it has been purified. It is powerful because it knows the Source.

And even if God's plan does not include romantic restoration, love still abounds. Love takes the form of ministry, of friendship, of family, of self-compassion. The ashes of your pain become the soil of your purpose. What was once loss becomes legacy. Every healed heart becomes a vessel through which divine love flows freely into a hurting world.

God is not finished with your story. Every ember that remains from the fire will glow again with hope. The same Spirit that comforted you in sorrow will empower you to love courageously again—not because you've forgotten the ashes, but because you've discovered beauty beyond them.

Vignette: The Garden After the Fire

After her husband's sudden passing, Denise swore she'd never love again. She poured her energy into her church and her garden. One summer, a lightning storm struck and burned part of her backyard, leaving behind a patch of scorched earth. Heartbroken, she considered paving it over.

But the next spring, something unexpected happened—flowers bloomed in that same spot, brighter than before. The fire had released nutrients into the soil that made new growth possible. Denise wept as she realized: *God can bring beauty from even this.*

Years later, she met a widower named Charles at a grief ministry event. They became friends, then prayer partners, then something deeper. When she married again, she chose to hold the ceremony in her garden—right where the fire once burned.

Love had not replaced what was lost; it had redeemed it. What once was ashes becoming altar.

Reflection: The Courage to Love Again

To love again after loss is one of the bravest acts of faith. It requires opening the heart God just healed. But courage in love is not about risk;

it's about trust. You're not trusting people blindly—you're trusting God completely.

Ask yourself: *Am I protecting my heart or imprisoning it?* Healing gives you permission to hope again. Don't confuse walls for wisdom. It's possible to guard your peace while still allowing love to find you.

Love after ashes reminds us that grace doesn't just rebuild—it restores joy. You can live again, laugh again, and love again without fear, because the One who healed you now holds you.

Life Application: Living and Loving After Loss

1. **Let God define your worth.** Before stepping into new love, make sure your identity rests in Christ, not in companionship.

2. **Forgive what burned you.** Release those who hurt you. Forgiveness frees your heart for fresh affection.

3. **Learn from your ashes.** Don't bury the lessons of the past—use them to recognize God's standards in the future.

4. **Embrace timing, not tension.** Don't force what's meant to unfold. Let God orchestrate introductions and confirmations.

5. **Keep love sacred.** Whether it's friendship, ministry, or marriage, let your love glorify God first and fulfill you second.

Love reborn through grace doesn't rush—it rests. It doesn't perform—it prays. It doesn't chase—it chooses peace.

Closing Prayer

Redeeming God, Thank You for teaching me that love does not end in loss. Heal every place in me that has been scorched by pain. Restore hope where disappointment lived. Teach me to love from a healed heart—with courage, patience, and discernment. If You call me to love again, let it be a reflection of Your grace. May my life testify that beauty truly can rise from ashes. In Jesus' name, Amen.

Appendix I — Devotional Companion: Love Beyond the Ashes

Key Scripture: *"To grant to those who mourn in Zion—to give them beauty for ashes, the oil of joy for mourning, the garment of praise for the spirit of heaviness."*— **Isaiah 61:3 (NKJV)**

Purpose of this Devotional:

God never ends your story in ashes. This devotional companion invites you to rediscover love — for yourself, your calling, and for others — through God's power to redeem what was lost and renew what remains.

Day 1 — The God Who Rebuilds

Scripture: Nehemiah 2:18

Reflection: God restores what's broken one stone at a time. He never rebuilds the same — He builds stronger.

Practice: Write down one area of your life you sense God is rebuilding.

Prayer: *Lord, thank You for being the Architect of my new beginning.*

Day 2 — Beauty Rising from the Ashes

Scripture: Isaiah 61:3

Reflection: God trades ashes for beauty, but the exchange requires surrender. When you let go of what burned, you make room for what blooms.

Practice: Light a candle today and thank God for turning your darkest moments into light.

Prayer: *Father, I praise You for the beauty emerging from my pain.*

Day 3 — Learning to Love Again

Scripture: 1 Corinthians 13:13

Reflection: After loss, love feels risky. But real love is not reckless; it's redeemed.

Practice: Pray for God to heal the part of your heart that fears love.

Prayer: *God, renew my capacity to give and receive love without fear.*

Day 4 — The Healing Power of Gratitude

Scripture: 1 Thessalonians 5:18

Reflection: Gratitude shifts the focus from what was lost to what was left. Praise transforms pain.

Practice: List three things you're thankful for today — even in transition.

Prayer: *Lord, teach me to see Your hand even in what hurts.*

Day 5 — Redeemed Love Restores Worth

Scripture: Luke 7:47

Reflection: The forgiven love deeply. Knowing how much grace has covered you births compassion for others.

Practice: Reach out to someone walking through loss. Offer words of hope.

Prayer: *Jesus, help me to love others as generously as You've loved me.*

Day 6 — When Love Looks Different

Scripture: John 21:15–17

Reflection: Peter's love changed after failure; it matured. God teaches us to love again in new ways after disappointment.

Practice: Reflect on how your understanding of love has deepened through pain.

Prayer: *Lord, refine my love so that it reflects Your patience and grace.*

Day 7 — Joy Restored, Heart Renewed

Scripture: Psalm 30:11–12

Reflection: The joy that returns after sorrow is stronger, sweeter, and sure.

Practice: Sing or hum a song of praise that reminds you of God's faithfulness.

Prayer: *Thank You, Father, for turning my mourning into music and my ashes into adoration.*

Love after loss is one of the most courageous journeys a believer can take. From the counseling chair, I have seen individuals wrestle with questions that reach far beneath the surface:

- "Can I love again without betraying my past?"
- "Can my heart handle another disappointment?"
- "Will I ever feel whole enough to open myself again?"
- "Is it even possible to trust after such pain?"

This chapter addresses the emotional and spiritual readiness required to receive love after ashes.

Pastoral Counseling Lens - From the Counseling Chair

1. Trauma Recovery: Understanding Why the Heart Hesitates

Loss—whether through death, divorce, betrayal, or abandonment—leaves a mark.

Many carries unspoken thoughts such as:

- "If I love again, I might lose again."
- "I can't survive another heartbreak."
- "Something must be wrong with me."

Trauma recovery begins by acknowledging that fear is a *normal* emotional response to deep pain.

Scripture provides this assurance: "**He gives beauty for ashes...**" (Isaiah 61:3)

God does not minimize grief—He redeems it.

2. Cognitive Reframing: Love After Loss Is Not Replacing—It Is Renewing

The mind can sabotage new beginnings with distorted beliefs:

- "New love dishonors old love."
- "My past disqualifies my future."

- “Happiness is dangerous.”
- “If things feel good, they will inevitably fall apart.”

CBT reframing rewrites these misbeliefs:

Old Thought: “Moving forward means I’m letting go of what was valuable.”

Reframed Truth: “God can honor your past and still bless your future.”

Old Thought: “Love is too risky.”

Reframed Truth: “God equips the heart to love with wisdom.”

Old Thought: “The ashes are all I have left.”

Reframed Truth: “The ashes are the soil where new love can grow.”

3. Attachment Strengthening: Learning Secure Love After Wounded Love

Ashes often distort attachment:

- Abandonment creates hypervigilance,
- Betrayal creates distrust,
- Rejection creates emotional walls,
- Unresolved grief creates emotional numbness.

Therapeutically, individuals learn:

- The difference between discernment and fear,
- How to trust again in stages,
- How to identify safe love,
- How to recognize emotional red flags,
- And how to rebuild relationship patterns rooted in security rather than panic.

Spiritually, love becomes safer when grounded in identity, not insecurity.

"**Perfect love casts out fear.**" (1 John 4:18)

4. Grief Integration: Carrying Memory Without Carrying Weight

Grief does not disappear—it gets integrated.

Healthy integration looks like:

- Remembering without reliving,
- Honoring without idolizing,
- Grieving without sinking,
- Opening the heart without erasing what came before.

Jesus Himself honored grief with tears (John 11:35). He shows us that grieving and loving again are not enemies—they are companions.

5. Forgiveness Work: Releasing the Ashes That Weigh the Heart Down

Unforgiveness makes the heart heavy. Before new love can flourish, individuals often must release:

- Bitterness from betrayal,
- Guilt from past decisions,
- Self-blame that lingers,
- Anger at God for allowing the loss,
- Disappointment in themselves or others.

Forgiveness lifts the spiritual weight that keeps love from breathing.

"Let all bitterness... be put away from you." (Ephesians 4:31)

Forgiveness is oxygen for the heart.

6. Emotional Readiness: Assessing When the Heart Is Prepared to Love Again

Love is not a race—it is a rhythm.

In counseling, I guide individuals through "readiness checkpoints" such as:

✓ Can you remember your past without emotional collapse?

✓ Can you speak honestly about what hurt without blaming yourself?

✓ Can you imagine a future with hope?

✓ Can you differentiate a new person from past pain?

✓ Can you trust God with the timing of release and restoration?

When these answers shift from *fear* to *faith*, love is no longer a threat—it becomes a possibility.

7. Discernment: Recognizing Redeemed Love vs. Repeated Patterns

Not every opportunity for love is sent by God.

Discernment helps individuals recognize:

- Emotional health vs. Emotional dependency
- God-sent love vs. Trauma-bonded connections
- Fruit-bearing relationships vs. Fantasy-based attachments
- Healing love vs. Hurried love

Silent seasons deepen a person's ability to hear the Holy Spirit's guidance.

Redeemed love is patient, wise, measured, and Spirit-led.

8. Scriptural Anchoring: God Writes Restoration Stories

Every therapeutic principle aligns with Scripture:

- **Trauma Recovery** → "He restores my soul." (Psalm 23:3)
- **Cognitive Reframing** → "Behold, I will do a new thing." (Isaiah 43:19)
- **Attachment Strengthening** → "Underneath are the everlasting arms." (Deut. 33:27)
- **Grief Integration** → "Blessed are those who mourn…" (Matt. 5:4)
- **Forgiveness** → "Forgive seventy times seven." (Matt. 18:22)
- **Readiness & Discernment** → "My sheep hear my voice." (John 10:27)

God writes love stories beyond ashes—stories full of purpose, maturity, wisdom, and peace.

Pastoral Summary

From the counseling chair, I see "love beyond the ashes" not as replacing what was lost, but as **receiving what is redeemed**.

Love after loss is:

- A divine invitation,
- A sign of inner healing,
- A testimony of god's faithfulness,
- And a celebration of resilience.

True love does not erase ashes—it rises from them.

When God restores love, it is deeper, wiser, and more aligned with His heart for your wholeness.

Declaration:

I am loved beyond loss. My ashes have become altars of adoration. God's grace has made me whole, and love has been reborn within me.

Closing Benediction for the Week

"Weeping may endure for a night, but joy comes in the morning." — Psalm 30:5 (NKJV)

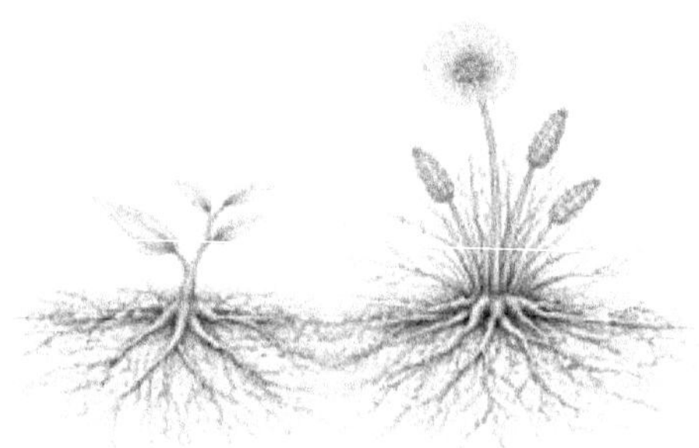

Chapter 10: "Whole and Holy"

"Now may the God of peace Himself sanctify you completely; and may your whole spirit, soul, and body be preserved blameless at the coming of our Lord Jesus Christ."— **1 Thessalonians 5:23 (NKJV)**

Exegetical Note:

Paul uses the Greek verb ***hagiasai*** ("sanctify") — meaning *to set apart for sacred purpose, to purify, to make whole.* Sanctification is not merely moral cleansing; it is **divine integration**.

The word *"completely"* translates the Greek term ***holotelēs*** — literally "entire in every part." It signifies **nothing missing, nothing fractured, nothing left unattended**. Paul is praying for wholeness that reaches every corner of one's being.

He then identifies the threefold makeup of humanity:

- **Spirit** (*pneuma*) — God-awareness
- **Soul** (*psychē*) — self-awareness (mind, will, emotions)
- **Body** (*sōma*) — world-awareness (earthly vessel)

Wholeness is not achieved through perfection, but through divine alignment — each part harmonized under God's peace.

Historical Context:

The church at Thessalonica was young, persecuted, and spiritually eager. They wrestled with fear, confusion about the future, and concerns about Christ's return. Paul writes to steady them, reminding them that holiness is not a frantic pursuit but a peaceful work of God Himself.

Unlike the legalism of the Pharisees, Paul's view of sanctification is relational: God sanctifies *with* us, *for* us, and *within* us.

He is not the God of partial healing or fragmented identity. He is the **God of peace** — the One who restores harmony where life created heaviness.

Pastoral Insight:

Wholeness is not perfection; it is peace in alignment. It is the maturity that comes from learning who you are in God, letting go of who you were in pain, and embracing who you are becoming in purpose.

Many believers pursue holiness while ignoring the fragmentation in their soul. But God sanctifies the whole person —the spirit that reaches upward, the soul that reaches inward, and the body that reaches outward.

To be whole and holy is to live integrated — with your identity, emotions, relationships, and faith woven together under God's loving rule.

This journey has taught us that:

- Spring restores hope,
- Summer strengthens endurance,
- Autumn refines surrender,
- Winter renews stillness.

And now, God invites you to step into a **new spring** —a season where healing becomes harmony and holiness becomes wholeness.

Wholeness is not who you were — it is who you are becoming in God's hands.

Wholeness is not perfection; it is peace. It is living authentically in the rhythm of grace. "Now may the God of peace Himself sanctify you completely; and may your whole spirit, soul, and body be preserved blameless at the coming of our Lord Jesus Christ" (1 Thessalonians 5:23 NKJV).

To be whole is to be integrated—spirit, soul, and body aligned under God's purpose. Many seek holiness apart from wholeness, but God desires both. Holiness is the surrender of self; wholeness is the healing that follows. When holiness and wholeness meet, peace takes residence in the heart. You begin to walk in a divine equilibrium—no longer fractured by fear, guilt, or comparison, but anchored in grace and guided by truth. Together, they create a life marked not by flawlessness, but by fullness.

Wholeness is not the absence of struggle; it is the presence of stability. It means that even when life shakes, your foundation in Christ holds firm. You may bend, but you will not break. You may cry, but you will not collapse. Wholeness is the quiet assurance that you are complete in Christ, even as you continue to grow. It is the ability to rest in God's love without constantly striving for validation. When you know who you are in Him, you stop chasing what cannot complete you. You begin to live not for applause, but from acceptance in Him. Your strength comes not from your own striving, but from the quiet assurance that God has completed what He began in you. "He who has begun a good work in you will complete it" (Philippians 1:6 NKJV).

As this journey closes, may I remind you that every season has purpose: spring prepared you, summer grew you, autumn refined you, and winter restored you. Now a new spring dawns—one marked by peace, gratitude, and renewed calling. The cycles of becoming have not ended they evolved and matured. You are not who you were when this journey began. You are wiser, softer, stronger, and more surrendered. Each season adds a layer of wisdom, beauty, and depth to the soul.

Living whole means living aware: aware of God's presence, your worth, and your mission. It means no longer being defined by what happened to you but by what God is doing through you. Wholeness is the courage to live healed. You see your scars as reminders, not regrets. You view your life as a testimony, not a tragedy. Wholeness invites you to walk confidently in your identity as a beloved child of God, fully restored and purposefully redeemed.

Wholeness also calls for stewardship. It asks, "How will you now live?" The healed heart must become a healing vessel. What God did *in* you; He now desires to do *through* you. Whole people build healthy relationships, lead with empathy, and serve with integrity. Wholeness isn't just for personal peace—it's for Kingdom impact.

Holiness is what keeps wholeness from becoming self-centered. It anchors peace in purpose. Holiness says, "Lord, not my will, but Yours be done." It's the sacred rhythm of humility that ensures your healing serves heaven's agenda. When holiness sanctifies your wholeness, your life becomes a living altar—an offering of gratitude, obedience, and worship.

When you live whole and holy, you become a living testimony of restoration. Your presence becomes ministry. Your peace becomes proof. People may not know your story, but they'll sense your strength. The light that shines through you will not come from perfection, but from presence—the presence of God resting upon a life surrendered and sanctified.

You are not the same person who began this journey. You have walked through change, endured the heat, released the unnecessary, and rediscovered peace in silence. You have been healed, pruned, and prepared. What once wounded you has now become your witness. What once limited you now lifts you. You are living proof that broken things in the hands of God become beautiful beyond measure.

To live whole and holy is to live free. Free from the need for perfection. Free from the weight of shame. Free to love boldly and forgive quickly. Free to live with open hands, trusting that God will fill them again and again. Freedom in Christ does not erase your past—it redeems it. The same God who brought you through each season will continue to lead you with wisdom and grace.

You may not have understood every part of the process, but God wastes nothing. Every disappointment was shaping your discernment. Every loss was cultivating your compassion. Every waiting season was developing your worship. You have journeyed through the cycles of life and emerged not empty, but expectant. This is what it means to be whole—to find contentment in His care, courage in His calling, and calm in His sovereignty.

Wholeness is not the end—it's the evidence. It shows that every season has fulfilled its purpose. Holiness is not pressure—it's privilege. It shows that your life has become an offering of gratitude to the One who brought you this far.

Let this be your declaration: *I am whole—not because life is perfect, but because grace is sufficient. I am holy—not because I am flawless, but because I am forgiven. I am at peace—not because I have everything, but because I have Him.*

As one season ends and another begins, may you walk in divine confidence, clothed in peace and crowned with purpose. You are living proof that brokenness can be restored, that endings can birth beginnings, and that God's faithfulness is greater than any season you face.

Vignette: The Mirror at the Retreat

During a women's retreat, the facilitator handed each participant a small mirror. "I want you to look at yourself," she said softly, "and see what God sees."

Most women hesitated. Some wept. For years, they had only seen the reflection of failure, regret, and pain. But one woman—Angela—felt the Spirit whisper, *"You are whole. You are holy. You are Mine."*

Tears streamed as she lifted her head for the first time without shame. The mirror no longer showed what life had taken—it showed what grace had restored.

Later that evening, she shared her story with the group: "I came here broken, but I'm leaving whole. And the best part? My holiness isn't in my perfection—it's in my surrender."

The room grew still. What she said was simple, yet sacred. Holiness and wholeness had met—and peace filled the space.

Reflection: Living in Divine Balance

Wholeness and holiness are not opposites—they are companions. Wholeness grounds you; holiness guides you. One keeps your heart healed; the other keeps your life aligned. Together, they make you complete.

Ask yourself: *Am I living from peace or striving for it?* If peace feels far away, pause and remember: peace is not found in perfection—it's found in presence. When you rest in the awareness that you belong to God, striving ceases, and surrender begins.

To live whole and holy is to live from overflow. You no longer love out of emptiness, serve out of exhaustion, or forgive out of obligation. You live from fullness, and that fullness is Christ in you—the hope of glory.

Life Application: Walking Whole and Holy

1. **Prioritize soul alignment.** Each day, bring your spirit, soul, and body under God's authority through prayer and reflection.

2. **Pursue purity of purpose.** Ask, "Why am I doing this?" Let love, not ambition, be your motivation.

3. **Protect your peace.** Don't let people or pressures pull you out of spiritual balance. Guard your emotional boundaries with grace.

4. **Practice consistency.** Small, daily acts of obedience lead to lifelong transformation.

5. **Praise continually.** Gratitude anchors wholeness. Make thanksgiving your daily rhythm.

Peace is maintained by perspective. When your focus stays on God, your heart stays whole.

Closing Prayer

Faithful Father, Thank You for the journey that has led me to wholeness. Thank You for sanctifying every season—teaching me through pain, strengthening me through silence, and restoring me through grace. Help me to live each day in balance—spirit, soul, and body in harmony with Your will. Let my life reflect Your holiness and my heart remain whole in Your love. May peace be my portion, and purpose be my path. In Jesus' name, Amen.

Appendix J — Devotional Companion: Whole and Holy

Key Scripture: *"Now may the God of peace Himself sanctify you completely; and may your whole spirit, soul, and body be preserved blameless at the coming of our Lord Jesus Christ."*— **1 Thessalonians 5:23 (NKJV)**

Purpose of this Devotional:

Day 1 — Peace as a Person

Scripture: John 14:27

Reflection: True peace is not a feeling; it is the presence of Christ. Wholeness begins when we stop chasing calm and start embracing Christ Himself.

Practice: Sit quietly and name one area where you need Christ's peace.

Prayer: *Jesus, be my peace today. Still my heart with Your presence.*

Day 2 — Spirit, Soul, and Body

Scripture: Proverbs 4:23

Reflection: God cares for every part of you. Wholeness means tending to your spirit (faith), soul (emotions), and body (habits). Neglect in one area disrupts balance in all.

Practice: Choose one area to nurture today—prayer, journaling, or rest.

Prayer: *Lord, align my spirit, steady my soul, and strengthen my body.*

Day 3 — Sanctified by Surrender

Scripture: Romans 12:1

Reflection: Holiness begins where striving ends. When we surrender our plans, pressures, and personas to God, He restores what trying could not touch.

Practice: Pray a simple prayer of release: "Lord, I give You everything again."

Prayer: *Father, sanctify my life through surrender. I yield all to You.*

Day 4 — Living Integrated

Scripture: James 1:8

Reflection: A divided heart cannot carry divine purpose. Integration means your walk matches your worship and your identity matches your calling.

Practice: Identify one place where you feel divided—and ask God for unity.

Prayer: *God, make me whole. Unite the parts of me that feel scattered.*

Day 5 — The Holy Rhythm of Rest

Scripture: Psalm 23:2–3

Reflection: Rest is not laziness—it is obedience. God restores your soul when you stop long enough to breathe.

Practice: Take at least 10 minutes today to rest intentionally.

Prayer: *Shepherd of my soul, lead me beside still waters again.*

Day 6 — Blameless but Not Perfect

Scripture: Philippians 3:12

Reflection: God calls us to walk blameless—not flawless. Blamelessness is consistency, humility, and repentance. Perfection is not the goal; purity of intention is.

Practice: Confess one area where you desire growth.

Prayer: *Lord, perfect what concerns me. Shape my heart, correct my course.*

Day 7 — Becoming God's Reflection

Scripture: 2 Corinthians 3:18

Reflection: Wholeness is the lifelong process of looking more like Jesus. Not suddenly—but steadily. One degree of glory at a time.

Practice: Ask God to transform one attitude, reaction, or mindset today.

Prayer: *Holy Spirit, transform me from the inside out.* Wholeness and holiness are not destinations—they are lifelong journeys. From the counseling chair, I've learned that many believers strive for spiritual perfection while neglecting emotional integration. Others pursue emotional healing without inviting the Holy Spirit into the process. But true wholeness—the kind that manifests peace, clarity, resilience, and authenticity—comes when **spiritual formation and emotional health meet under the lordship of Christ.**

This chapter explores the beautiful relationship between healing, holiness, and the integration of one's entire being—spirit, soul, and body.

Pastoral Counseling Lens - From the Counseling Chair

1. Identity Integration: Becoming One Person in All Places

Many individuals live fragmented lives:

- Spiritually strong but emotionally exhausted
- Outwardly accomplished but inwardly insecure
- Relationally present but internally disconnected
- Forgiven by God but unable to forgive themselves

Wholeness means becoming the same person in every room—integrated, congruent, and anchored in Christ.

Scripture affirms this integration: "**May your whole spirit, soul, and body be preserved blameless…**" (1 Thessalonians 5:23)

In counseling, identity integration involves:

- Aligning your self-talk with Scripture
- Bringing hidden parts of the heart into God's light
- Embracing both strength and vulnerability
- Allowing God to heal the parts that perfectionism hides
- Breaking agreement with shame

Holiness is not behavior modification—it is identity transformation.

2. Cognitive Renewal: Sanctifying the Thought Life

Wholeness requires mental sanctification—renewing the mind so that thoughts align with truth rather than trauma, fear, or negative core beliefs.

Common internal misbeliefs include:

- "If people knew the real me, they wouldn't love me."
- "God is disappointed in me."
- "I'm too damaged to be used by God."
- "My past disqualifies my calling."

CBT, when infused with Scripture, transforms these into truth:

- *"I am fully known and deeply loved."*
- *"There is no condemnation for those in Christ."*
- *"God's strength is made perfect in my weakness."*
- *"Nothing can separate me from God's love."*

Holy thinking produces holy living.

3. Emotional Maturity: Holiness in How We Feel and Respond

Holiness is not only about what we avoid—it's about how we manage the inner world God entrusted to us.

Emotionally mature believers:

- Process emotions without suppressing them
- Communicate with clarity rather than aggression
- Allow the holy spirit to regulate internal storms
- Respond with grace instead of reactivity
- Practice forgiveness as a lifestyle
- Maintain boundaries that honor God and self

Scripture supports emotional maturity: "**Let the peace of God rule in your hearts.**" (Colossians 3:15)

Whole hearts do not manipulate, lash out, or collapse under pressure—they remain grounded in God's peace.

4. Holiness Through Healing: God Uses Wounds as Worship

Some believe holiness means never struggling—but the opposite is true.

Holiness is:

- Bringing your broken places to God
- Choosing surrender over self-sufficiency
- Embracing healing instead of hiding
- Repenting without self-hatred
- Walking in freedom rather than fear

Your wounds become testimonies when placed in God's hands. Holiness deepens when healing is embraced.

5. Forgiveness & Release: Clearing the Soul for Spiritual Renewal

Wholeness cannot exist where bitterness abides. In counseling, I often see individuals held hostage by:

- Resentment
- Old betrayals
- Internalized shame
- Regret over past choices
- Disappointment with God or self

Forgiveness is a spiritual detox. Scripture anchors this command: **"Forgive as Christ forgave you."** (Colossians 3:13)

Forgiveness is not minimizing pain—it is maximizing peace.

Once forgiveness flows:

- Joy returns
- Clarity rises
- Purpose emerges
- Holiness is restored
- Emotional weight falls away
- Wholeness requires a cleared soul.

6. Boundary Setting: Holiness With Wisdom, Not Weakness

Many Christians equate boundaries with selfishness. In counseling, I teach that boundaries are both holy and healthy.

Jesus Himself practiced boundaries:

- He withdrew from crowds to rest
- He chose inner-circle relationships
- He said "no" to demands that didn't align with His mission
- He protected His purpose

Healthy boundaries support wholeness because they:

- Prevent emotional depletion
- Protect spiritual focus
- Reduce relational conflict
- Promote self-respect
- Cultivate peace

Boundaries are an expression of stewardship.

7. Spiritual Discipline: Sustaining Wholeness Through Daily Practices

Wholeness is maintained through spiritual rhythms:

- Consistent prayer

- Meditating on scripture
- Worship
- Silence and solitude
- Sabbath rest
- Gratitude journaling
- Serving others
- Spiritual community

These disciplines shape the heart into Christ's image.

Holiness grows in consistency, not intensity.

8. Scriptural Anchoring: God Desires Both Wholeness and Holiness

Every therapeutic principle in this chapter is rooted in Scripture:

- **Identity Integration** → "You are God's workmanship." (Eph. 2:10)

- **Cognitive Renewal** → "Be transformed by the renewing of your mind." (Rom. 12:2)

- **Emotional Maturity** → "Be slow to anger." (James 1:19)

- **Healing as Holiness** → "By His stripes we are healed." (Isaiah 53:5)

- **Forgiveness** → "Love keeps no record of wrongs." (1 Cor. 13:5)

- **Boundaries** → "Guard your heart…" (Prov. 4:23)
- **Spiritual Discipline** → "Abide in Me…" (John 15:4)

God doesn't want you just healed—He wants you **whole and holy**.

Pastoral Summary

From the counseling chair, I define wholeness as a life lived in alignment—emotionally, spiritually, mentally, relationally, and purposefully.

Wholeness is:

- Living with peace instead of pretense
- Walking in identity instead of insecurity
- Embracing healing instead of hiding
- Thinking truth instead of trauma
- Loving from abundance instead of emptiness
- Choosing holiness with joy, not pressure

Holiness is not perfection—it is being set apart for God's use. Wholeness is not flawlessness—it is being fully present, fully surrendered, and fully available to God.

You are becoming whole and holy—not by striving, but by surrendering to the God who completes every good work.

Declaration

I am whole in His presence. I am holy by His grace. My life is aligned, my spirit is anchored, and my purpose is maturing. Wholeness is my portion. Holiness is my path. I walk in the peace of God—fully, freely, and faithfully.

Closing Benediction for the Week

"The Lord will perfect that which concerns me."— Psalm 138:8 (NKJV)

Epilogue New Spring: A Season of Renewal

Spring always returns. No matter how long the winter has felt, no matter how silent the nights or how heavy the snow of your circumstances, God is faithful to send a new season. This truth echoes throughout Scripture and reverberates through every page of this book: **God writes resurrection into every story surrendered to Him.**

New spring is not simply the end of suffering—it is the beginning of *becoming again.*

A Season of Reawakening

Just as the earth awakens after winter's stillness, your spirit rises from seasons of silence, grief, or transition. What felt buried is now breaking forth. What seemed dormant is quietly stirring beneath the surface. The same God who breathes life into dormant trees is breathing fresh strength into your soul.

"**Behold, I will do a new thing; now it shall spring forth.**"—Isaiah 43:19 (NKJV)

New spring is God's gentle reminder that nothing in Him is wasted—not the heartache, not the lessons, not the tears, not the waiting.

A Season of New Identity

Every winter strips us of something we once clung to: a title, a role, a relationship, a dream. But spring doesn't return what was lost—it reveals who you are *now*. You are wiser. You are rooted. You are healed in places you didn't know were fractured. You carry grace that was forged in the fire and wisdom that was shaped in the silence.

You have learned:

- To release without collapsing,
- To forgive without forgetting the lesson,
- To wait without losing hope,
- To trust without needing constant reassurance,
- And to love without losing yourself.

You are stepping into this new spring as someone God has redesigned from the inside out.

A Season of New Growth

Spring teaches us the beauty of slow, steady growth. What emerges first are small signs:

- Joy returning in simple moments,
- Hope rising without fear,
- Peace settling where anxiety once lived,
- Renewed purpose unfolding step by step.

You may not feel fully whole yet—but beloved, you are growing.

God does not rush seasons, He cultivates them and He is cultivating you.

A Season of New Calling

Every chapter of this book has echoed a single truth: **wholeness is not passive—it is purposeful.** New spring carries an invitation to:

- Serve with deeper compassion,
- Love with clearer boundaries,
- Lead with greater humility,
- And walk with a renewed sense of calling.

Your winter did not disqualify you—it prepared you.

It sharpened your discernment. It refined your character. It strengthened your faith. It deepened your reliance on God.

Now you rise—not as who you were, but as who God has shaped you to become.

A Season of Renewal

You have journeyed through:

Spring — The Season of Becoming

Summer — The Season of Growth

Autumn — The Season of Release

Winter — The Season of Stillness

And now, as you prepare to close this book, know this: You are standing on the threshold of a new beginning.

Becoming is not a one-time event. Wholeness is not a single destination. Marriage Holiness is not a fixed point.

Each new spring invites you to become again—with deeper trust, greater wisdom, and renewed faith.

Chapter 11: Pastoral Q&A

Sacred Conversations for the Journey

Throughout my years of ministry and counseling, I have learned that people rarely come asking questions simply to gain information. More often, they come seeking permission—to feel, to grieve, to hope again, and to believe that God is still at work in their lives.

The conversations that follow are not answers shouted from a distance, but sacred exchanges whispered along the journey. They reflect the seasons in which God meets us, shapes us, and gently calls us toward wholeness.

1. "How do I protect my faith during seasons of emotional pain?"

Pain does not destroy faith—but unprocessed pain can distort it.

Faith grows strongest when anchored in **truth**, not **feelings**.

Ways to protect your faith in painful seasons:

1. **Stay connected to community.**

Isolation intensifies pain. Support stabilizes faith.

2. **Keep a simple prayer life.**

Pain makes deep prayers hard—but short, honest prayers still move heaven.

3. **Speak Scripture over your emotions.**

Your feelings are real, but God's Word is final.

4. **Take your questions to God, not away from Him.**

God is not intimidated by your "why." He invites your honesty.

5. **Practice gratitude in small doses.**

Gratitude lifts the heart where bitterness tries to take root.

6. **Give yourself permission to heal slowly.**

Faith grows strong in-patient soil.

Scripture Anchor:

"The righteous cry out, and the Lord hears…"—Psalm 34:17 (NKJV)

Your faith is safest when it is honest.

2. "How do I handle loneliness in any season—single, married, divorced, remarried, renewal, or grieving?"

Loneliness is not a sign of weakness; it is a sign of humanity. Even Jesus said, "*My soul is exceedingly sorrowful, even unto death.*" (Matthew 26:38)

Loneliness shows up when:

- Needs are unmet
- Support systems shift
- Relationships change
- The heart outgrows its old environment

Loneliness is an emotional signal—not a spiritual deficiency.

Three truths about loneliness:

1. **Loneliness often precedes revelation.**

Moses was alone at the burning bush. Elijah heard God in silence. Jacob wrestled alone before his name changed.

Your isolation may be an invitation.

2. **Loneliness does not mean God is absent.**

"The Lord is close to the brokenhearted." (Psalm 34:18)

He sits with you in the silent spaces.

3. Loneliness can become a place of restructuring.

Use this time to:

- Reconnect with purpose
- Rediscover your identity
- Re-evaluate boundaries
- Re-engage spiritual disciplines

Counseling lens: Loneliness signals that connection is needed; it does not mean connection is impossible.

3. "How can a person find fullness and satisfaction in singleness?"

In a culture that treats marriage as the ultimate goal, singleness can feel misunderstood—but in Scripture, **singleness is not a deficiency. It is a divine calling, a complete season, and a place of spiritual strength.**

God does not measure your worth by marital status. He measures it by **devotion, purpose, and obedience**.

Singleness in God's sight is not loneliness—it is **wholeness**, stewardship, and availability to Him.

I share this not as theory, but as lived truth. After divorce, I remained **celibate for nearly two decades**—not because it was easy, but because obedience mattered more than urgency. That season taught me that fullness does not come from companionship, affection, or attention; it comes from **alignment with God**. Celibacy did not diminish my life—it clarified it. It deepened my prayer life, strengthened my discernment, healed my heart, and anchored my identity in Christ rather than in relationship status.

4. "What if I've done everything 'right' and I'm still single?"

Answer:

This is one of the most painful and honest questions a believer can ask. Scripture never teaches that obedience guarantees a particular outcome—only that it secures God's presence within the process.

Doing "everything right" does not mean God has overlooked you. It often means He has been forming you deeply, shaping your discernment, strengthening your faith, and preparing you for responsibilities you may not yet see.

Singleness is not proof of delay, deficiency, or disfavor. It may simply be evidence that God is more committed to your wholeness than to your timetable.

Waiting is not wasted when God is involved.

5. "How do I deal with sexual desire in a season of celibacy?"

Answer:

Sexual desire is not sinful—it is God-given. The issue is not desire itself, but stewardship of it. Celibacy is not the denial of desire; it is the disciplined direction of it.

Celibacy requires honesty, not suppression. Desire must be acknowledged, prayed through, and brought under the authority of God rather than managed in secrecy or shame.

Healthy practices during celibacy include:

- Honest prayer without guilt
- Clear boundaries that protect the heart and body
- Spiritual disciplines that redirect energy
- Accountability with trusted, godly support

Celibacy is not about punishment—it is about alignment. And when lived faithfully, it produces clarity, strength, and spiritual maturity.

6. How to Experience Fullness in Godly Singleness?

1. Know that singleness is a gift, not a limitation.

Paul called it a *charisma*—a grace-gift (1 Corinthians 7:7). Not because it is easy, but because it provides spiritual freedom and focus unmatched in other seasons.

2. Anchor your identity in Christ—not companionship.

Your worth is not measured by who chooses you but by Who created you. Identity settles insecurity.

3. Pursue purpose with intentionality.

Singleness offers undivided time, energy, and emotional bandwidth to build, grow, serve, travel, study, create, and thrive. Purpose makes life rich—even before partnership.

4. Cultivate deep spiritual intimacy.

Singleness allows you to build a relationship with God that is not divided by competing responsibilities. This intimacy becomes your greatest source of joy.

5. Build meaningful community.

God did not create you for isolation. Friendships, ministry circles, and godly mentors become your support system and spiritual family.

6. Practice contentment without complacency.

Contentment says, "I am whole now." Complacency says, "I'll never hope again." God invites you to both enjoy the present and remain open to His future plans—whatever they may be.

7. Use this season to heal, grow, and become whole.

Marriage does not erase wounds. Singleness is often where God does the deepest inner work—work that strengthens every future season.

Scripture Anchor:

"I have learned in whatever state I am, to be content…I can do all things through Christ who strengthens me."—Philippians 4:11, 13 (NKJV)

Contentment is not a circumstance—it is a *strength* Christ provides.

And also:

"The unmarried cares for the things of the Lord, how he may please the Lord."—1 Corinthians 7:32 (NKJV)

God sees singleness as a season of availability, intimacy, and spiritual power—not a waiting room.

7. "What does God want me to learn in my single season?"

Singleness is not a waiting room—it is a classroom.

Lessons God often teaches:

1. **Identity**

   Learning who you are without external validation.

2. **Purpose**

   Discovering your assignment before entering partnership.

3. **Healing**

   Addressing patterns that relationships tend to cxposc.

4. **Stewardship**

   Learning how to guard heart, time, and emotions.

5. **Intimacy with God**

   Your greatest relationship begins vertically before it becomes horizontal.

"In all thy ways acknowledge Him…"—Proverbs 3:6

Singleness is not a punishment. It is preparation.

8. "What is the difference between dating and courting?"

Courtship—not dating—is the clarion call for Christians.

Dating in today's culture is often casual, emotional, and undefined. It prioritizes chemistry over covenant, pleasure over purpose, and connection over character. Dating asks, *"Do we enjoy each other right now?"* Courtship asks, *"Are we spiritually aligned for a future in Christ?"*

Key differences:

1. **Dating is recreational; courtship is purposeful.**

   Dating seeks companionship. Courtship seeks clarity.

2. **Dating centers on emotions; courtship centers on God's will.**

   Dating follows feelings. Courtship follows faith.

3. **Dating lack's structure; courtship has boundaries.**

   Dating often removes accountability. Courtship welcomes it—pastors, mentors, and community.

4. **Dating tests compatibility; courtship examines calling.**

Dating asks if you "fit." Courtship asks if you "match purpose."

5. **Dating encourages exploration; courtship encourages consecration.**

Dating opens hearts quickly. Courtship guards' hearts intentionally.

9. Why courtship is the Christian standard?

Courtship honors holiness. It protects purity. It keeps God—not desire—at the center.

Courtship invites the Holy Spirit into every step, from conversation to commitment. It recognizes that marriage is sacred, and therefore, the pathway to marriage must also be sacred.

Scripture Anchor:

"Keep your heart with all diligence, for out of it spring the issues of life."—Proverbs 4:23 (NKJV)

Courtship protects the heart. Dating exposes it.

What are healthy boundaries in Christian courtship?"

Boundaries are not barriers—they are **biblical safeguards** that keep the relationship holy, healthy, and Spirit-led. Courtship thrives when purity and purpose guide every decision.

Healthy Boundaries Include:

1. Spiritual Boundaries

- Pray together, but not in isolation that breeds emotional entanglement.
- Keep Christ—not chemistry—as the center.
- Invite pastoral covering or godly mentors into the journey.

2. Emotional Boundaries

- Share gradually, not prematurely.
- Guard deep intimacy until covenant commitment is clear.
- Do not rely on the other person for emotional rescue—God is your first refuge.

3. Physical Boundaries

- No secret spaces, late-night environments, or prolonged physical closeness.

- Purity is not about restriction—it's about protection.
- Honor God with your body and each other's dignity.

4. Communication Boundaries

- Be honest without oversharing wounds prematurely.
- Keep conversations encouraging, uplifting, and aligned with your courtship goals.
- Don't promise what God has not confirmed.

5. Time Boundaries

- Balance courtship with ministry, friendships, work, and personal growth.
- Don't isolate from the life God has already given you.

Scripture Anchor:

"This is the will of God, your sanctification: that you should abstain from sexual immorality… and possess your own vessel in sanctification and honor."—**1 Thessalonians 4:3–4 (NKJV)**

Boundaries are a form of worship—they help you honor God while guarding your heart.

10. "How do we rebuild trust after betrayal?"

Trust is not rebuilt through apology—it is rebuilt through consistency.

Scripture says, "**By their fruits you will know them.**"—Matthew 7:20

Three phases of rebuilding trust:

1. **Transparency**

- No secrets
- No hidden communication
- Open devices
- Full honesty
- Transparency restores safety.

2. **Accountability**

- Counseling
- Check-ins
- Support systems
- Personal repentance
- Accountability restores integrity.

3. **Consistency**

- Daily proof of change
- Changed patterns, not promises

- Softened tone, not sharp excuses
- Consistency restores confidence.

Counseling lens: Betrayal wounds the attachment system. Healing requires predictable patterns that rebuild emotional safety over time. Trust is not rebuilt quickly, but with humility, accountability, and a surrendered heart—it *can* be restored.

11. "How do I know if staying is faith—or fear?"

Answer:

Faith and fear can look similar on the surface, but they produce very different fruit.

Faith is anchored in peace, even when the path is difficult. Fear is sustained by anxiety, guilt, or obligation. Faith draws you closer to God; fear leaves you depleted, isolated, and spiritually constricted.
Ask yourself:

- Does staying align with God's character and wisdom?
- Is there evidence of growth, repentance, or movement?
- Am I choosing endurance out of conviction—or avoidance?

God never asks His children to remain in situations that destroy their dignity, safety, or spiritual health. Faith is not endurance without discernment.

When unsure, seek God in prayer and invite wise, biblical counsel. Truth becomes clearer in the presence of light.

12. "What if my life doesn't look like what I prayed for?"

Answer:

Few experiences challenge faith more deeply than unanswered or altered prayers. Yet God's faithfulness is not measured by how closely life follows our expectations.

Sometimes God answers prayer by **reshaping the person who prayed**. A life that looks different from what you envisioned is not necessarily a life without purpose. God often fulfills prayers in ways that are **truer, deeper, and more enduring** than we imagined.

Wholeness is not found in having everything turn out as planned—it is found in trusting that God remains present, purposeful, and faithful in every season.

13. How do I stay married when I feel like giving up?"

Marriage is a covenant—but covenants come with seasons of testing. Wanting to give up does not make you weak or unspiritual. It makes you **human**.

The real question is not, "Do I feel like staying?" but **"How can I honor God while my emotions are overwhelmed?"**

Scripture does not command us to "feel" married—it commands us to *fight for unity*, pursue peace, and seek God's help in weakness.

Staying married requires **wisdom, willingness, and spiritual work**, not perfection.

14. What to do when you want to walk away?

1. **Slow down—don't make permanent decisions in temporary emotions.**

Feelings fluctuate. Covenants do not. Give God space to speak before you step.

"**Be still, and know…**" (Psalm 46:10)

2. **Seek God before seeking an exit.**

Prayer won't fix everything instantly, but it will fix *your posture*—and posture shapes perspective.

3. **Invite wise, biblical counsel—don't struggle in secret.**

Marriage was never meant to be fought for alone. Reveal the struggle to a pastor, Christian counselor, or mature believer.

Isolation intensifies pain. Community stabilizes it.

4. Identify the real enemy.

Your spouse is not the opponent. Your emotions are not the enemy. Spiritual warfare is real, and the enemy hates covenant.

5. Work on the heart behind the hurt.

Ask:

- What part of me is reacting?
- What wound is being triggered?
- What need is going unmet?
- What pattern keeps repeating?

Marriage problems are often symptom problems.

6. Rebuild connection in small but sincere steps.

Sometimes God restores through:

- One act of kindness
- One honest conversation
- One counseling session
- One prayer together
- One apology
- One reset

Restoration rarely arrives in a wave. It arrives in a series of small obedience's.

7. Examine whether you are exhausted or truly finished.

Exhaustion can feel like "I want out." But exhaustion is treated; hopelessness is addressed; and God heals both.

Sometimes the issue is not the marriage—it is the *weariness*.

"He restores my soul."

15. "Why does the devil try to separate what God has joined together?

When God joins two lives together in covenant, there will always be opposition. Jesus made it clear that marriage is not merely a legal agreement—it is a divine joining.

"What therefore God hath joined together, let not man put asunder." (Mark 10:9)

If God joins it, the enemy targets it.

1. Recognize the source of the attack.

Not every conflict is relational—some are spiritual. Satan does not need to destroy love; he only needs to distort it through pride, offense, silence, and division.

"For we wrestle not against flesh and blood…" (Ephesians 6:12)

2. Guard unity as a spiritual discipline.

Unity does not happen naturally; it is protected intentionally. Unity requires humility, repentance, forgiveness, and prayer.

Division is the enemy's favorite tool—but unity is heaven's defense.

3. Resist the lie that separation will bring peace.

Temporary relief is not the same as lasting healing. The enemy often offers escape when God is offering endurance, growth, and transformation.
God heals through covenant, not always around it.

4. Cover your marriage in prayer, not just conversation.

Some battles cannot be talked through—they must be prayed through. Prayer shifts the atmosphere, disarms the enemy, and re-centers God as the third strand in the union.

"A threefold cord is not quickly broken." (Ecclesiastes 4:12)

5. Remember why God joined you in the first place.

God does nothing accidentally. What He joined, He joined with purpose—beyond romance, beyond seasons, beyond struggle.

When hell tries to separate, heaven calls you to stand.

Pastoral Reminder:

Every covenant will be tested. Tests do not mean the covenant is failing—they reveal whether it is being fought for spiritually or only emotionally.
What God has joined, fight for in prayer, protect with wisdom, and trust with faith.

16. When separation or safety is needed?

Staying married does **not** mean staying in harm's way.
Scripture never commands a person to endure:

- Abuse
- Threats
- Violence
- Unsafe conditions

Safety is stewardship. Leaving danger is not abandoning covenant—it is protecting God's creation.

Even in those cases, decisions must be made with counsel, clarity, and covering.

Scripture Anchor:

"Let nothing be done through selfish ambition or conceit, but in lowliness of mind let each esteem others better than himself."—**Philippians 2:3 (NKJV)**

"Love bears all things, believes all things, hopes all things, endures all things."**—1 Corinthians 13:7 (NKJV)**

These verses are not burdens—they are **strength** for weary hearts.

17. "When reconciliation isn't possible, how do I release well?"

Sometimes peace requires separation. Paul wrote, "If it is possible, as much as depends on you, live peaceably with all men."**—Romans 12:18**

Notice: *if it is possible.* Some situations are not.

To release well:

1. **Release without revenge.**

You cannot heal and retaliate at the same time.

2. **Release with clarity.**

Close the door God closed—don't keep peeking through the window.

3. **Release with boundaries.**

Distance is protection, not punishment.

4. **Release with forgiveness.**

Forgiveness is not reconciliation. Forgiveness frees *you*; reconciliation requires *their involvement*.

5. **Release with God's peace.**

God does not call you to remain where wholeness cannot grow.

Counseling lens: Releasing is a grief process. Treat it with the tenderness you would give any other loss.

18. "How do I explain my season to my children with hope?"

Children thrive on emotional clarity. They don't need details—they need direction.

Tips:

Use simple truth.

"Mommy and Daddy are in a healing season." God is helping our family grow in a new way."

1. **Normalize emotions.**

   "It's okay to feel sad or confused. God is with us."

2. **Provide reassurance.**

   "You are loved." "This is not your fault." "We are stable and safe."

3. **Keep spiritual hope alive.**

   "We believe God is guiding our family." "He never leaves us."

4. **Keep adult details for adults.**

   Children are not emotional caretakers.

   Counseling lens: Children don't need you to be perfect—they need you to be predictable.

19. "Is God disappointed in me if I'm divorced?"

Absolutely not. God is not surprised by your humanity; He is committed to your healing.

Psalm 34:18 says, "**The Lord is near to the brokenhearted.**"

Divorce is not God's original design, but neither is:

- Abuse
- Betrayal
- Abandonment
- Addictions

- Manipulation
- Irreconcilable harm

God meets you *where you are,* not where people think you should be.

He forgives. He restores. He renews.

Divorce does not disqualify your destiny—God redeems every season.

20. "What does God say about remarriage?"

Remarriage is a subject that must be approached with **grace, Scripture, and truth**. The Bible does not forbid remarriage—but it does give **conditions, counsel, and clarity** so that we walk in wisdom and honor God in every season.

Remarriage is not a "lesser" marriage, scripture shows that **God restores, rebuilds, and renews**. Many faithful believers experience new covenant love after seasons of loss, divorce, or widowhood.

The key is this: **God blesses remarriage when it is done in righteousness, healing, and discernment.**

21. What the Bible Teaches About Remarriage:

1. **Remarriage after widowhood is clearly affirmed in Scripture.**

The Bible encourages widows and widowers to remarry if they desire. Paul said: "**She is at liberty to be married to whom she wishes, only in the Lord.**"—1 Corinthians 7:39 (NKJV)

Widowhood does not disqualify you from future love. God honors covenant—and He also comforts the brokenhearted.

2. **Remarriage after divorce is permitted when the marriage covenant has been biblically broken.**

Jesus and Paul both acknowledge that there are situations in which the covenant is dissolved and remarriage is allowed.

The two primary biblical grounds are:

Sexual immorality (Matthew 19:9)

Adultery breaks covenant trust and may release the innocent spouse. Jesus said: "**Whoever divorces... for sexual immorality...**" — indicating that this is a recognized ground for release.

Abandonment by an unbelieving spouse (1 Corinthians 7:15)

If an unbelieving spouse departs and refuses reconciliation, Paul says: "**The brother or sister is not under bondage in such cases.**"

This "not under bondage" means **free from the marriage covenant**—and therefore free to marry again "in the Lord."

3. **Remarriage must follow genuine healing, not just desire.**

Even when Scripture allows it, God calls us into remarriage with a healed heart, renewed mind, and spiritual maturity.

Remarriage should never be:

- An escape from loneliness
- A rebound from pain
- A reaction to pressure
- A search for emotional rescue

It must be **prayerful, peaceful, and Spirit-led**.

4. **Remarriage must be "in the Lord."**

Paul emphasizes this phrase (1 Cor. 7:39) because remarriage is not simply starting over—it is entering covenant again under **God's order, holiness, and guidance**.

A God-honoring remarriage reflects:

- Spiritual alignment
- Emotional health
- Mutual purpose
- Shared values
- Christ-centered love

5. **God does not shame believers who remarry.**

Divorce creates wounds, but it does *not* remove God's grace. Scripture does not teach that remarried people are second-class Christians. Jesus met the woman at the well—five marriages behind her—yet He offered **living water**, not condemnation (John 4:1–26).

Remarriage in righteousness is a picture of God's:

- Redemption
- Renewal
- Restoration
- Compassion

God restores what life tries to break.

Scripture Anchor:

"**Behold, I make all things new.**"—Revelation 21:5 (NKJV)

And:

"He restores my soul." Psalm 23:3 (NKJV)

God not only permits restoration—He *delights* in restoring His people.

22. "What if my season does not match the season of the person I'm courting or married to?"

Seasons rarely align perfectly. One partner may be:

- In spring (becoming)
- While the other is in winter (stillness)
- Or autumn (letting go)
- Or summer (growth)

When seasons differ, remember:

1. **Maturity requires empathy.**

Understand the season your partner is in. Ask, "How can I support your growth without losing mine?"

2. **Emotional timing affects relational timing.**

Partnership is not about matching pace—it's matching purpose.

3. **Communicate seasonally.**

Say: "Here's where my heart is right now…" "Here's what I'm processing…" "Here's what I need in this season…"

4. **Do not force someone out of their season.**

You cannot rush healing. You cannot hurry becoming. You cannot push someone into readiness.

5. **Ask God for unified vision.**

Alignment is more important than identical pace.

"**Can two walks together unless they agree?**"—Amos 3:3

Unity is not sameness—it is surrendering your seasons to God together.

23. "How do I maintain faith when God's timing feels slow?"

Waiting on God is not passive—it is **active trust**. Every season of waiting is a classroom where God teaches dependence, patience, and spiritual resilience.

"Those who wait on the Lord shall renew their strength…"—**Isaiah 40:31 (NKJV)**

If the timing feels slow, it is because the **preparation is deep**.

Signs you're learning to trust God's timing:

1. You choose worship instead of worry.

Worship recenters your heart and puts God back on the throne of your emotions.

2. You surrender the desire to control outcomes.

Control creates anxiety. Surrender creates peace.

3. You look for God's hand in the small things.

He often works quietly before He moves visibly. Pay attention to subtle shifts—they are signs of divine progress.

4. You remain faithful where you are.

God finishes developing you in the current season before He promotes you to the next one.

5. You trust that delay is not denial.

Delay is often protection, preparation, or redirection. God is not slow—He is strategic.

Scripture Anchor:

"Write the vision… though it tarries, wait for it; because it will surely come, it will not tarry."—Habakkuk 2:2–3 (NKJV)

God's timing may feel slow, but it is always precise, purposeful, and perfect.

24. "How do I know the difference between pruning and quitting?"

Pruning is God-initiated; quitting is fear-initiated. Pruning removes what blocks growth. Quitting removes what discomforts us.

Jesus teaches: **"Every branch that bears fruit He prunes, that it may bear more fruit.**"—John 15:2 (NKJV)

Pruning produces:

- Discomfort but not destruction
- Conviction but not condemnation
- Temporary loss but long-term increase
- Clarity, alignment, and fruit

Quitting produces:

- Regret
- Unresolved wounds
- Avoidance
- Emotional shutdown
- Spiritual stagnation

Counseling lens: Ask yourself:

- *Is God trimming what no longer serves my purpose?* (pruning)

- *Or am I walking away to avoid healing, accountability, or growth?* (quitting)

A practical marker: If God is leading you *toward* holiness, wholeness, emotional maturity, and clarity—this is pruning. If you feel driven by fear, shame, resentment, or exhaustion—this may be quitting.

Pruning hurts, but quitting harms Pruning makes room for more; quitting makes room for nothing. Ask God honestly, "What are You trying to grow in me through this?"

25. "How do I know when God is redirecting my steps in ministry?"

Redirection is not about leaving something—it is about leaning into what God is preparing next. When the Lord shifts your assignment, He does it with clarity, consistency, and peace.

1. You sense a repeated stirring from the Holy Spirit.

When the same prompting returns during prayer, worship, or reflection, God may be preparing your heart for a new season. He leads with conviction, not confusion.

2. You feel a holy restlessness—not frustration.

Restlessness with purpose often signals growth. It is the inward sense that God is calling you to stretch, develop, or serve differently.

3. Your gifts are expanding beyond your current lane.

As God grows you, He enlarges your capacity. New burdens, new passions, and new opportunities often point toward a fresh assignment.

4. Your current season feels complete.

"There is a time for every purpose…" (Ecclesiastes 3:1) Completion is not conflict; it is a quiet release that says, "This season has fulfilled its purpose."

5. God opens doors you did not seek out.

Divine redirection is confirmed by alignment: unexpected invitations, new ministry roles, and opportunities that fit your gifting and calling.

6. Mature counsel affirms what God is showing you.

"By the mouth of two or three witnesses…" (2 Corinthians 13:1) Trusted spiritual voices often confirm what the Holy Spirit has already spoken.

7. Peace becomes stronger than fear.

Where God guides, He supplies peace. If fear is loud but peace is louder—transition may be God-led.

Scripture Anchor:

"The steps of a good man are ordered by the Lord…"— Psalm 37:23 (NKJV)

When God redirects your steps, He confirms it through His Word, settles it with His peace, and proves it with fruit.

Closing Pastoral Blessing

Every season carries questions—but none carry condemnation. May you trust the God who meets you in the asking, walks with you in the waiting, and leads you faithfully toward wholeness in every season.

www.ingramcontent.com/pod-product-compliance
Ingram Content Group UK Ltd.
Pitfield, Milton Keynes, MK11 3LW, UK
UKHW020144250726
13967UKWH00002B/849

9 781967 086412